Privileged Access Management

Strategies for Zero Trust in the Enterprise

Gregory C. Rasner
Maria C. Rasner

Apress®

Privileged Access Management: Strategies for Zero Trust in the Enterprise

Gregory C. Rasner
Clayton, NC, USA

Maria C. Rasner
Clayton, NC, USA

ISBN-13 (pbk): 979-8-8688-1430-3
https://doi.org/10.1007/979-8-8688-1431-0

ISBN-13 (electronic): 979-8-8688-1431-0

Copyright © 2025 by Gregory C. Rasner, Maria C. Rasner

Managing Director, Apress Media LLC: Welmoed Spahr
Acquisitions Editor: Susan McDermott
Development Editor: Laura Berendson
Project Manager: Jessica Vakili

Distributed to the book trade worldwide by Springer Science+Business Media New York, 1 New York Plaza, New York, NY 10004. Phone 1-800-SPRINGER, fax (201) 348-4505, e-mail orders-ny@springer-sbm.com, or visit www.springeronline.com. Apress Media, LLC is a Delaware LLC and the sole member (owner) is Springer Science + Business Media Finance Inc (SSBM Finance Inc). SSBM Finance Inc is a **Delaware** corporation.

For information on translations, please e-mail booktranslations@springernature.com; for reprint, paperback, or audio rights, please e-mail bookpermissions@springernature.com.

Apress titles may be purchased in bulk for academic, corporate, or promotional use. eBook versions and licenses are also available for most titles. For more information, reference our Print and eBook Bulk Sales web page at http://www.apress.com/bulk-sales.

If disposing of this product, please recycle the paper

We dedicate this book to our kids. This book is proof that you can achieve anything with hard work, dedication, and the love of your family.

Table of Contents

About the Authors

Gregory C. Rasner (CISSP, CIPM, ITIL, CCNA) is the founder and CEO of Third Party Threat Hunting LLC, bringing his unique and extensive knowledge of third-party, supply chain, and cybersecurity risk to the market. He is the author of the books *Cybersecurity & Third-Party Risk: Third Party Threat Hunting* (Wiley, 2021) and *Zero Trust and Third-Party Risk* (Wiley, 2023) and the content creator of the training and certification program "Third Party Cyber Risk Assessor (TPCRA)" (Third Party Risk Association, 2023). He frequently serves as a keynote speaker and panelist on topics related to cybersecurity and risk management, along with writing blogs, podcasts, and online articles. Greg was the SVP and Leader for Cyber Third-Party Risk at Truist Financial Corp., and he received his BA from Claremont McKenna College. He is also actively engaged in leadership roles with cybersecurity and third-party risk task forces, boards, and industry groups.

Maria C. Rasner (CISM, CCSK, CCZT, ITIL) has extensive experience in Identity and Access Management (IAM) and Privileged Access Management (PAM). She has run governance, operations, remediation, implementation, and large IAM and PAM programs at small to large enterprises. Her experience and certifications include cloud certifications in Microsoft and AWS and implementation of PIM in the cloud. Maria has published several articles in the ISSA online journal and the Identity Defined Security Alliance (IDSA). Maria is passionate about mentoring others and has been part of her organization's WIT (Women in IT) program to help empower women to achieve their career goals in IT. Maria currently works for a large US bank as an IAM leader.

About the Technical Reviewer

Jerry Chapman is a cybersecurity professional with a focus on identity. With over 25 years of industry experience, Jerry has successfully guided numerous clients in the design and implementation of their enterprise IAM strategies, in ways that align with both security and business objectives. His job roles have spanned enterprise architecture, solution engineering, and software architecture and development. Jerry is active in the technical working group at the Identity Defined Security Alliance (IDSA), where he was the group's original technical architect. Jerry is a certified Forrester Zero Trust Strategist and has a BS in Computer Information Systems from DeVry University. Finally, Jerry is a coauthor of the renowned book *Zero Trust Security: An Enterprise Guide*.

Acknowledgments

First, we give thanks to the Lord for giving us the ability to write this book. We'd like to acknowledge our technical reviewer, Jerry Chapman, for his help to make it a better book. Thanks to the Apress team for their work to get it all across the finish line.

CHAPTER 1

Privileged Access Management: The Essentials

Chapter Overview

In this chapter, we will cover an overview of Privileged Access Management (PAM) to ensure all readers are on the same page as we dive into this topic much more profoundly. We will define what a privileged account is and then discuss more advanced topics, such as just-in-time access and session management. Starting with an introduction to PAM will allow us to level-set with all readers to ensure that as we progress into more advanced topics, the basics are covered.

We will cover Identity and Access Management (IAM) and PAM basics, the risk of elevated accounts, some terminology, PAM architecture, and the implementation steps to provide some itemized lists to assist the reader.

© Gregory C. Rasner, Maria C. Rasner 2025
G. C. Rasner and M. C. Rasner, *Privileged Access Management*,
https://doi.org/10.1007/979-8-8688-1431-0_1

The four steps for successful PAM implementation are as follows:

1. Discovery

2. Governance

3. Monitor and Audit

4. Automate

The four steps of a successful PAM life cycle are as follows:

1. Define and Discover

2. Onboarding

3. Monitor and Audit

4. Offboarding

These are the Magnificent Seven PAM Best Practices:

1. Enforce MFA

2. Cross-platform support

3. Temporary elevated access (TEA)

4. Segregation of duties (a.k.a. separation of duties)

5. Role-based access control (RBAC)

6. Automate

7. Maintain and monitor

Privileged Access Management combines people, processes, and technology to drastically lower the risk of elevated accounts.

Introduction to PAM

Privileged Access Management (PAM), as described in the National Institute of Standards and Technology (NIST) 800-53, focuses on managing and controlling access to privileged accounts, permissions, and servers to reduce the risk of unauthorized access, misuse, or abuse.[1] However, it would be best to start by explaining what "privileged" is and what it is not. "Elevated" is another word often used for privileged (elevated access = privileged access). It is defined by the National Institute of Standards and Technology as "a user that is authorized (and therefore, trusted) to perform security-relevant functions that ordinary users are not authorized to perform."[2] Note that "therefore, trusted" hits a key term in Zero Trust. Because a privileged user is by definition "trusted," the process and controls around Privileged Access Management are critically important to get right to get Zero Trust right.

Introduction to IAM

This book assumes some familiarity with Identity and Access Management. However, it is essential to cover some of the IAM basics. Identity and Access Management is a large area that covers technical and business processes for controlling access. PAM is a subsection or part of an overall IAM program, generally. Identity is key to success in any Zero Trust deployment and essential in a Privileged Access Management program. Whether your identity management systems are centralized or spread out (as is typical with many modern organizations), ensuring you have a well-run and operating IAM program will drive both PAM and Zero Trust success.

---

[1] https://nvlpubs.nist.gov/nistpubs/SpecialPublications/NIST.SP.
800-53r5.pdf
[2] https://csrc.nist.gov/glossary/term/privileged_user

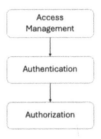

Figure 1-1. *Access Management Process*

Within IAM, there is a critical access management process. Access management is a two-step process: first, the process of the user or machine proving they are who they claim to be, which is called *authentication*; the second step is *authorization*, which establishes the actions and access the user or machine is able to perform. In the section "PAM and IAM Terms," we will define some of the ways authentication is performed:

- Certificate-based

- FIDO2

- LDAP

- OAuth2

- OpenID Connect (OIDC)

- RADIUS

- SAML

These authentication methods have challenges, but pay attention to legacy vs. newer protocols or procedures. For example, RADIUS is confined to single-factor authentication (SFA) and, therefore, is a particular challenge for PAM (which should require multifactor authentication) and Zero Trust strategy success.

In addition, during authentication, there are ways that can be performed. For example, normal users have to submit their username and password. This is single-factor authentication (SFA). Administrators, executives, vendors, and privileged accounts are required to not only submit their username and password. They must also confirm with a key fob that randomly rotates numbers plus a known "seed" number from the user. This is multifactor authentication (MFA). Suppose the user is detected to be overseas or in an atypical geographic region. In that case, the system may request a "step-up authentication" in a one-time passcode (OTP) sent to their registered phone number. Lastly, getting to a passwordless authentication scheme is a worthy goal as it eliminates some of the most egregious risks with passwords (see authors' note below on passwords).

Authors' Note on Passwords

Passwords are frustrating. Let's get that out of our system. Users dislike them, and so do administrators. Administrators generally face longer password length and complexity rules, making it even more burdensome for them. Additionally, they must handle the consequences (a breach) when a user neglects their password discipline. This is the most significant risk of passwords: human laziness. Most users choose the easiest passwords to remember, as we all have too many to juggle. A user will select a simple word to remember and then recycle it by doing the following: "Password", "Password1", "Password2", etc. What we describe above, the recycling of passwords, is what some organizations do to get around this laziness: by imposing a password history on users. This requires them to not use the same password for a specific set number of times. However, there should also be a minimum password age set for the domain. Usually, this is one day. This is because if there is no minimum age, then a user will cycle through the minimum history required and then arrive back at their original password.

Taking the example above, let's say the organization has a password history of ten, a password age of no more than 90 days, but no minimum password age set. The user can do this when prompted to change it at 89 days: currently, their password is "Password", so they type in "Password1", "Password2",... "Password10" and then arrive back at "Password" as their password for the next 90 days. This negates any password rotation when no minimum password age is set.

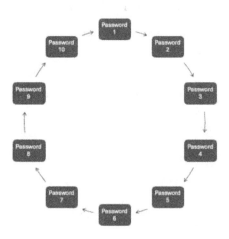

Figure 1-2. *Password History and Rotation*

Authorization is the goal of the access management process, designed to ensure that users or machines receive the appropriate access to the right resources at the right time. It should involve roles and attributes to determine the level of access. These roles and attributes are linked to entities governed by risk and compliance (GRC) standards to ensure their accuracy.

Privileged Account Risk

What is the risk of privileged accounts? Privileged accounts, with elevated access, are accounts where the user has the rights to Create, Edit, Update, Delete (CRUD) objects and resources that a user of this same object or resource doesn't have. These accounts present a direct risk in access to protected data and systems. These elevated accounts with privileged rights require extra processes, people, and technology to lower the risk of a breach.

Let's start with some numbers to clarify the risk elevated accounts pose to the enterprise:

- 74% of breaches involved access to a privileged account.[3]

- 87% of local administrators are not enrolled in a privileged account management solution.[4]

- 21% of administrators use default account names.

- 90% of security professionals said they experienced an identity-related incident in the past year.[5]

- 76% of cloud accounts for sale on the dark Web are for RDP access.[6]

- 62% of administrators admit to not changing passwords in more than one year.

---

[3] https://securis.com/news/privileged-access-management/
[4] https://cybermagazine.com/articles/privileged-access-securing-cybercrimes-most-coveted-target
[5] IDSA, 2023 Trends in Securing Digital Identities, May 30, 2023
[6] IBM Security, 2022 IBM Security X-Force Cloud Threat Landscape Report

- 40,000+ types of cloud permissions to manage.[7]

- In 99% of pen-testing cases, cloud identities were found to be overprivileged.[8]

  - 98% of security professionals say the number of identities is increasing, primarily driven by cloud adoption, third parties, and machine identities.[9]

  - 74% of all breaches are a result of humans, via privilege misuse, stolen credentials, social engineering, or error. Three of these four reasons are user identity attacks that are managed in PAM.

  - 95% of machine identities are overprivileged.[10]

  - Tenfold increase in attempted password attacks from 2023 to 2024.[11]

  - 112% increase from 2023 to 2024 in dark web advertisements for access-broker services.[12]

  - Stolen credentials and phishing (to get those credentials) are two of the three primary ways bad actors gain access to an organization.[13]

---

[7] 2023 State of Cloud Permissions Risks Report, Microsoft Security, March 2023
[8] IBM Security, 2022 IBM Security X-Force Cloud Threat Landscape Report
[9] IBM Security, 2022 IBM Security X-Force Cloud Threat Landscape Report
[10] Gartner, Innovation Insight for CIEM, June 2021
[11] https://www.microsoft.com/en-us/security/security-insider/microsoft-digital-defense-report-2023
[12] https://go.crowdstrike.com/2023-global-threat-report
[13] https://www.verizon.com/business/resources/T851/reports/2024-dbir-data-breach-investigations-report.pdf

- 45% of remote users admit to using the same password for work and personal accounts.[14]

- In 54% of all cyberattacks in 2022, initial access was obtained with compromised credentials.[15]

- US$4.45 million is the average cost of a breach. This is up 15% in the last three years.[16]

- US$4.62 million is the average cost of a breach caused by stolen or compromised credentials.

- 328 days (11 months) is the average time to identify and contain breaches caused by stolen or compromised credentials compared to the overall mean time to identify and contain of 277 days (9 months).

- Considering that most breaches stem from insufficient PAM, we could compile the remaining 200 pages with examples, but that would make for dull reading. Here are some notable instances of incidents, events, and breaches where a lack of Privileged Access Management contributed to the occurrence:

- Yahoo, 2013 and 2014: Due to the lack of PAM controls, the attackers were able to exfiltrate the data of over one billion users, which included email addresses, birth dates, and phone numbers.

---

[14] https://expertinsights.com/insights/50-identity-and-access-security-stats-you-should-know/

[15] https://www.cisa.gov/sites/default/files/2023-07/FY22-RVA-Analysis%20-%20Final_508c.pdf

[16] https://www.ibm.com/reports/data-breach

- Target, 2013: The root cause of the breach of customer credit card data was the hackers elevating their accounts, due to lack of a privileged account management process. This resulted in the loss of 110 million customer credit card data.

- Anthem, 2015: The root cause of the breach of 80 million customers data was a stolen administrator credentials. Theft of credentials happens all the time, but with a proper PAM program running, they would have had no use in the breach that happened at Anthem.[17]

- Equifax, 2017: The root cause of the breach was a vulnerability in their web application that lacked any PAM. This allowed the bad actors to easily escalate their privileges and download the data of millions of customers.

- Uber, 2022: The root cause is two-fold; first was the attacker used "MFA fatigue", where they bombarded the subject with so many fake MFA requests; the user relented and sent them credentials. The second was hard-coded administrator credentials to the PAM system used at Uber. This was discovered by the attacker in a script left on the network. They had a PAM technology but not a sound PAM program that would have prevented or vastly lowered the risk of these events happening in the first place.

---

[17] https://www.oneidentity.com/community/blogs/b/privileged-access-management/posts/the-risks-of-not-implementing-privileged-access-management-in-your-organization

- GitHub, Ongoing: Because of its popularity as a public repository that encourages collaboration, this platform is rife with examples where organizations leverage this platform and do not leverage an appropriate PAM to ensure lack of incident, event, or breach.[18]

Considering the statistics listed above, it is clear that the risk is as elevated as the accounts we're trying to better manage and protect. Leveraging a Privileged Access Management solution that utilizes people, processes, and technology dramatically lowers the risk of an incident, event, or breach and reduces a threat actor's ability to access your protected systems.

PAM and IAM Terms

Any introduction to a large topic, such as Privileged Access Management, requires an explanation of several terms and acronyms to ensure all readers share the same terminology and taxonomy for this field. Some of these items will be part of larger discussions in later sections and chapters. Depending on your skill level and exposure to the Identity and Access Management (IAM) space, you can choose to review as much or as little of this list as needed:

- Adaptive Authentication: Where authentication policies are implemented or triggered based upon conditions (such as device type, level of the user, or current location).

---

[18] https://aembit.io/blog/real-life-examples-of-workload-identity-breaches-and-leaked-secrets-and-what-to-do-about-them-updated-regularly/

- API Access Management: Application programming interfaces is a set of functions and procedures allowing the creation of applications that access the features or data of an operating system, application, or other service.

- Attack Surface: Think of this as the surface area where any bad actor can target. This can be a zero-day vulnerability, bad policy, poor implementation, or human error (or all of those and others not listed).

- Attribute-Based Access Control: Where access is assigned based on the user, resource attributes, and environment.

- Authentication: Process to determine if a user is who they claim to be.

- Authentication Factors: (1) Something you are (fingerprint, retina), (2) something you have (two-factor token fob), (3) something you know (a password or one-time code), and some places will accept (4) someplace you are (a specific location).

- Authorization: The process to determine whether an identity is allowed to get access to a resource or service.

- Biometrics: The use of something you are factor—retina, face, fingerprint, palmprint, etc.

- Brute Force Attack: A method of attack where a bad actor attempts all possible combination of inputs (usually in an access attack, the attacker uses a dictionary of potential passwords, for example) to crack open access.

- Certificate Authority (CA): Is a trusted entity that validates the identities of items such as websites and email addresses.

- Certificate Management: Is a process of monitoring and managing the life cycle of certificates (typically X.509 certificates) and how they are being used, renewed, and expired.

- Deprovisioning: The process of removing access for a user from a system. When a user or employee leaves an organization, their access is removed.

- Enterprise Password Vault: These tools and technologies lower fatigue by automating PAM processes such as password generation, rotation, monitoring, and deletion.

- Federated Identity: Where multiple systems share identity data via a larger centralized system. In an enterprise network, a federated system would allow branch offices to manage their own systems while it is centrally controlled from a central computer system.

- FIDO2: The FIDO Alliance developed FIDO Authentication standards based on public key cryptography for authentication that is more secure than passwords and SMS OTPs, simpler for consumers to use, and easier for service providers to deploy and manage. FIDO Authentication enables password-only logins to be replaced with secure and fast login experiences across websites and apps.[19]

---

[19] https://fidoalliance.org/fido2/

- Fine-Grained Authorization (FGA): This level of granularity allows for more flexibility in systems that require complex permissions.

- Identity as a Service (IDaaS): A variation of Software as a Service (SaaS) where identity management is outsourced to a cloud platform, rather than running it in-house.

- Identity and Access Management (IAM): Process of placing users and groups to be able to access resources and addresses authentication, authorization, and access control.

- Identity Sprawl: When users have different identities spread out across an enterprise that are not synchronized.

- Least-Privileged Access: Lowering the Attack Surface by limiting access and privileges to only those required to perform functions required.

- Lightweight Directory Access Protocol (LDAP): A protocol for interacting with a hierarchical directory service database for authentication and authorization.

- Multifactor Authentication (MFA): Two or more "factors" used to ensure a user is authenticated. These are typically what you are, what you know, and what you have. Sometimes it can be where you are as well.

- OAuth 2.0: OAuth is an open standard that allows delegated access to user information. OAuth 2.0 is not backward compatible to OAuth 1.0.

- One-Time Passcode (OTP): When a code is sent from an identity system to a known contact point for that user to further validate the authentication step.

- OpenID Connect (OIDC): Is a RESTful authentication system that uses OAuth 2.0 for authorization.

- Passwordless Authentication: A term that applies to techniques that allow a user to authenticate without the use of a password, such as a biometric device.

  - Password Generator: These tools will suggest or require the use of a generated password rather than relying on the typically weak ones picked by humans.

  - Password Manager: Is a centralized, encrypted, and protected asset for securely storing and managing elevated credentials and some can provide processing of password handoffs.

  - Password Management: The process of securing and managing passwords during their life cycle from creation to deletion with governance, risk, and compliance overlay.

  - Phishing: A type of social engineering attack where the user is "tricked" by what seems like a real message that is used to steal credentials and lock systems up with encryption.

  - Privilege Elevation and Delegation Management (PEDM): Part of a Privileged Access Management process that allows non-administrator users to get temporary elevated access based upon process requirements.

15

- Privileged Access Management: A set of management principles that assist business to govern and secure privileged access and control when access can be given and to what or who and a process to manage and monitor adherence.

- Privileged Access Workstation: These are specially designated machines designed to ensure a layered security approach to access and resources.

- Privilege Escalation: A type of cyberattack in which a non-admin user is able to gain elevated or privileged account access via any number of means.

- Provisioning: Process of establishing an identity and associated access into a system. For example, when a new user registers for a new service or a new employee starts at a company and the user receives login credentials and chooses a password.

- Remote Authentication Dial-In User Service (RADIUS) is an authentication protocol. RADIUS is limited to username and password (single-factor authentication) due to its age and as such is unable to be used in modern systems attempting to achieve PAM and ZT success.

- Role-Based Access Control (RBAC): Is a concept where user permissions are assigned based upon the role in the organization. Having privileges assigned to roles is key to success in an RBAC-organized role.

- Security Assertion Markup Language (SAML): A standard protocol used to integrate authentication and authorization capabilities between multiple systems and is used as a way to perform Single Sign-On (SSO).

- Secrets: Refer to sensitive information like passwords, API keys, and other credentials that are used to authenticate and authorize access to systems and resources.

- Secrets Management: Process of storing, managing, and deleting access to credentials used by the enterprise.

- Service Accounts: These are very often privileged domain or local accounts that are used by critical services and infrastructure; they can execute batch files, run scheduled tasks, send data across application to application, update file systems, and more.

- Single Sign-On (SSO): Enables users to authenticate with multiple systems with a single authentication session. The most common use is in corporate enterprise networks where users only login once and authenticate but access multiple software systems.

- Step-Up Authentication: Process of requesting the user for another form of authentication based upon a trigger. For example, if it detects the user is overseas or trying to access an area of higher risk.

- Time-Based One-Time Password (TOTP): A generated code that is based on the current date and time along with a secret "seed" value.

- Two-Factor Authentication (2FA): Combination of two of the three authentication factors.

Some of these terms will be explained further in the subsequent sections and chapters. While it is not necessary to memorize these terms at this point, you should be familiar with them, as they are likely to be part of any discussion about Identity and Access Management and Privileged Access Management.

Least-Privileged Access

The core principle of PAM is least-privileged access. In NIST 800-53, Privileged Access Management focuses on adhering to the principle of least privilege. The principle of least privilege is a fundamental security concept that instructs organizations that users should have only the rights and permissions needed to perform their jobs. Access control professionals may sometimes take the easy way out by granting users more access rights than necessary to avoid the effort of determining the exact rights needed. This behavior undermines security and guarantees unauthorized access. Here are some statistics to demonstrate that least-privileged access is often not followed:

- 95% of machine identities are overprivileged.[20]

- In 99% of pen-testing cases, cloud identities were found to be overprivileged.[21]

The least-privileged access grants users the minimum access needed for their jobs. It restricts access to sensitive data and systems and segregates duties to ensure checks on each control are performed. The least privilege requires regular review and updates to users' access rights. Whether monthly, quarterly, or annually, there must be a process to review access to ensure rights have stayed the same.

---

[20] Gartner, Innovation Insight for CIEM, June 2021

[21] IBM Security, 2022 IGM Security X-Force Cloud Threat Landscape Report, 2022

Least-privileged access can be explained in simple terms by describing who has access to financial records in a bank. An accounts payable clerk can create a payment based on the process; however, they do not have the ability to view the full account profile for the business or entity.

Segregation of Duties (a.k.a. Separation of Duties)

Figure 1-3. *Segregation of Duties*

Segregation of duties is part of the least privilege principle in that no single user should have the ability to complete a critical business process or function by themselves. In the process of entering a new vendor into a procurement system, to avoid the potential for a fraudulent vendor being entered, two roles are necessary. The first role creates the data in the procurement system, but that record requires a second person to approve its addition and availability to accounts payable for sending money once services are rendered. In a Privileged Access Management process, this involves someone creating the elevated account in the Active Directory system and placing it in the appropriate group. An additional step involves another person who approves the granting of that privileged access to the user.

Dual Control

This is where two people approve the completion of a critical or sensitive business function. The immediate image that comes to mind for many in this instance is when, in the movies, a nuclear missile is fired; it requires two keys and two people to execute this incredible event. In the technology world, an example would be when it requires two administrators to delete an image on a backup tape or a webpage on the corporate site. In terms of least privilege and Privileged Access Management, it may be necessary to have dual control for the approval of certain highly critical and sensitive actions, such as opening "break glass" accounts or making changes to domain administrator accounts.

Figure 1-4. *Dual Controls*

Dual control is not the same as separation of duties. Dual control requires two people to approve a sensitive action, while separation of duties ensures no one person has ability to perform a sensitive action.

Separate Accounts

Critical to the success of least privilege and Privileged Access Management is having separate normal user accounts and elevated accounts for human users. No user should rely solely on their privileged account for access to any network or system. There must also be a "normal" user account for these individuals to use when they are not performing elevated tasks.

An example may help illustrate the need and why. A domain administrator in most organizations has enormous powers in the network. These accounts and users can make global changes to systems that could render the whole system inoperable and become an expensive doorstop.

However, 90% of the time, a domain administrator is not making these types of changes but is instead monitoring, measuring, or planning potential changes. Most of these activities do not require elevated access. All this time spent planning and monitoring is done in programs like word processing or dashboard screens in applications.

If a domain administrator is working on this type of non-elevated work, there is no need for them to be in the elevated account; they can and must work in a normal user account. This will ensure three critical things occur: First, they will not accidentally make a change in production while in this non-elevated account. Second, any change an elevated account can make (especially a domain administrator) should go through a change management process to capture the work being done. This restriction on making changes from a user account will ensure they properly follow the change management process. Finally, it will allow for better control over the times when the domain administrator needs to make changes that require elevated access. When they need to make a production change, they will be required to go through the organization's process to access the privileged account and perform the work.

Privilege Creep

This occurs when a user has been with an organization for a while in various roles. Ensuring that the user is stripped of any privileges they have as they leave a role is often overlooked in many organizations. For example, a person may start out as a database administrator, then get promoted to the manager of the database administrators; a few years later, they become a domain administrator supervisor. All of these roles have different levels of privileges and access to systems.

Figure 1-5. *Creeping*

As the person goes from position to position, their "old" access should be disabled (or deleted), and only their "new" role requirements should be enabled. The best methods for preventing this from happening are having regular access reviews and conducting them more frequently for privileged or elevated accounts. Minimum requirements for privileged account access reviews should be every 90 days.

Transitive Trust Creep

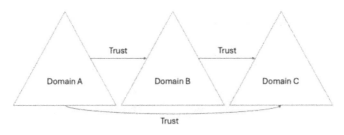

Figure 1-6. *Transitive Trust*

Much like the privilege creep previously described, access can be unintentionally granted by passing trust without awareness. For example, if Domain A trusts Domain B and Domain B trusts Domain C, then logically Domain A inherits the trust of Domain C. However, this trust relationship can usually be specified, so validating whether trust is two-way or inherited is critical to understand when evaluating controls and gaps. Assess and evaluate any trust relationships to comprehend the risk they pose to your privileged accounts.

Types of PAM accounts

There can be several typical types of elevated accounts. Typically, in an enterprise, there are **domain** and **local administrator** accounts. Domain administrators generally have the "key to the kingdom" for most or all enterprises. These accounts can change at the highest level in the enterprise down to most machines or systems within that enterprise. And these accounts are often the most sought after by the bad actors. Local administrators have much lower privileged access, usually limited to a single machine or server, but it can still be a high risk given what can run on a server. Often, these are pathways to elevated privileges for domain administrators.

Service accounts are also often privileged or elevated access. Service accounts are different from user accounts in that they are assigned to an application or service to allow them to operate and communicate. An application or program often needs more than read-only access; it often requires elevated permissions to perform required functions. Most applications or services will provide very descriptive access permissions their product requires upon installation. Pay attention to these requirements, and don't allow access to be given "domain admin" access. However, rights for the least-privileged access should be implemented.

Business privileged user accounts often belong to individuals who need elevated rights to perform administrative or managerial functions related to file locations, systems, and/or applications due to their job roles. This category also includes senior-level and C-suite staff, who typically possess enhanced privileges owing to their leadership positions. These accounts can be vulnerable to spear phishing, which is an activity wherein a malicious actor conducts a phishing campaign aimed at stealing these specific credentials.

Application administrator accounts are often easy targets these days because we are a software-driven society. Most organizations designate a person or more to perform administrator functions on applications to add/update user access or alter some settings in the software's back end. Often, accounts are left with default usernames and passwords, making them easy targets for threat actors using scripts and automated searches.

Emergency accounts often get forgotten because they are considered "break glass," referring to using them only in emergencies. These accounts are used in a disaster or some event that would prevent regular access for privileged users. An extreme example would be all your domain administrators quitting and not leaving you a way back into your system; this type of "break glass" or emergency account is the ticket to regain control. These accounts are elevated and require Privileged Access Management on them as well.

PAM Implementation (High-Level)

Implementing Privileged Access Management can be challenging, but here are four steps to break down the basic steps. There's a bit more to unpack in each of these steps, and we'll go through that in later chapters, but for now, this provides you with a way to organize it.

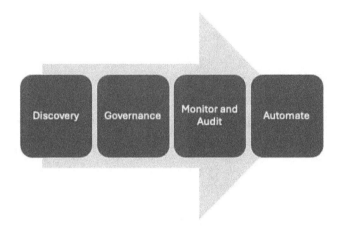

Figure 1-7. PAM Implementation

Discovery

Discovery is the step in which your organization finds out how significant the risk is in your enterprise. This process can be conducted in various ways, and none is necessarily better; however, it may be beneficial to try multiple methods to ensure everything is addressed. Using an automated tool to perform this step is preferred, as it is less likely to result in transpositional errors. However, not all organizations will have the financial capacity to access this type of tool. If it is a manual discovery process, make sure to have a clear definition of a privileged account, and include a step to validate each role with elevated access or rights.

Governance

Governance describes how your PAM will be operated and managed. The root of the word "govern" speaks to the intent of this area: to properly run and manage your organization's PAM process, people, and technology to ensure the process is repeatable and fully completed each time and that every individual involved knows their responsibility. If it is not written down (how your organization intends to govern this vital domain of PAM), then it is not being performed as expected every time. When there is no structure or guidance on how to perform activities, humans will decide on their own how to do them; the result is an ad hoc process that will miss essential steps and fail. Every. Single. Time. In later chapters, we will delve deeper into governance, but governance is a crucial step in any technology or process deployment, particularly Privileged Access Management.

Monitor and Audit

Once you've discovered and mapped all your PAM accounts and defined a governance structure, you need to monitor and audit these elevated access accounts in real time, as closely as your systems and personnel will allow. Monitor all accounts for their rights and access becoming privileged, and take action as your process describes for these accounts. Auditing involves having appropriate personnel review PAM accounts regularly (as described in your governance documentation) to ensure access is still necessary; otherwise, elevated access is removed as soon as possible to lower the risk.

Automate

Automate the implementation as much as possible, leveraging tools, technology, and/or personnel to ensure that the adoption of PAM is complete. Again, the definition of automate can be loose here and may not mean that your organization has it electronically automated but a process defined where people "automatically" step through the process on a regular (daily, weekly, monthly) basis to ensure adherence to the PAM implementation steps.

PAM Architecture

Architecture is defined in the Merriam-Webster online dictionary as "the manner in which the components of a computer or computer system are organized and integrated." It can also be described as the technique of designing how a system (computer, network, security) is to be built. An architect will create an architecture for an engineer to follow when they actually build or construct the computer, network, or security. It is important to start with an architecture in a complex system such as PAM to ensure completeness of coverage and provide engineers and operators of these systems with the ability to understand how they interact within the system.

This architecture comes from the National Cybersecurity Center of Excellence (NCCoE) and is designed to address the challenges of PAM across industries. The document referenced is an excellent reference for anyone looking for a two-pager on the risks of PAM and how to architect to fix it.

In Figure 1-8, what is noticeable is the gray box around the Privileged Access Management systems and policy. The Identity and Access Management system is outside of this where the Identity Store and multifactor authentication will occur for the PAM administrators and users to interface with the PAM area. Note that both PAM administrators and users would access PAM through a user interface that then talks (via Management Data Flow) to both the MFA and Identity Store systems as part of the process.

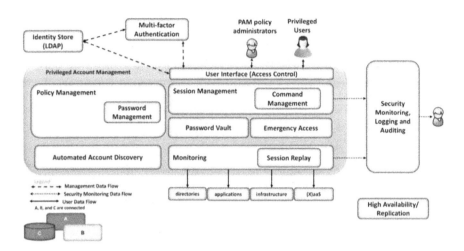

COMPONENT LIST

This solution includes, but is not limited to, the following components:

- privileged account control
- privileged account command filtering (allow or deny specific commands, such as disk formatting)
- multifactor authentication capability
- access logging/database system
- password management
- separation of duties management
- support least privileged policies
- password obfuscation (hiding passwords from PAM users)
- temporary accounts
- log management (analytics, storage, alerting)

Figure 1-8. *PAM High-Level Architecture*[22]

One of the missing labels is the one on the far right for the figure at the end of the Security Monitoring Data Flow. In most organizations, this action is not performed by a single person or unit. The group that manages the "Security Monitoring, Logging, and Auditing" often consists of several groups and, in some cases, may not even report to the same C-level organizations. For example, logging activity may be managed by the IT Operations teams under the Chief Information Office (CIO), while the consumer of the data, Security Monitoring, is run by the Security

---

[22] https://www.nccoe.nist.gov/sites/default/files/legacy-files/fs-pam-fact-sheet.pdf

Operations team under the Chief Information Security Office (CISO). This might explain why it was left blank, as it can be a single person in a very small organization, but more often than not, it involves multiple people and groups, necessitating a RACI matrix. A RACI matrix is a method for determining who or what is responsible for tasks being completed. Responsible, Accountable, Consult, and Inform are what the acronym stands for, and each term describes what each entity, group, or role must do for something to be completed.

The architecture is very basic, but that does not imply it is rudimentary. Basic, in this context, means it is designed to accommodate most organizations and is not overly complex, unlike many organizations and networks. In Figure 1-9, we observe what is likely representative of the complexity found in most organizations, as well as methods to address these challenges with innovative solutions, such as artificial intelligence and SOAR.

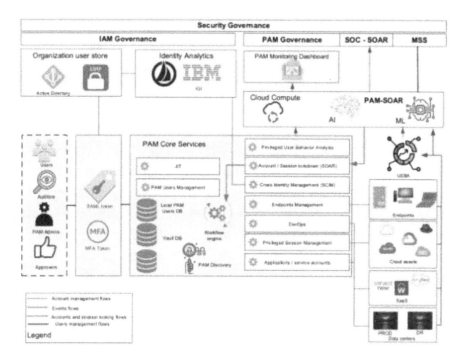

Figure 1-9. *PAM Future PAM Architecture[23]*

What immediately stands out on top of the overall graphic is a "Security Governance," and under that are "IAM Governance" and "PAM Governance." This elevation of the way these domains are "governed" is important because without that overlay, many organizations will not be consistent in both execution and review.

As part of session management and monitoring, another item of note is the level of detail in PAM Core Services to understand what is included in the offering and management core. SOAR, which stands for Security Orchestration, Automation, and Response, alleviates strain and missed opportunities by automating responses to events. SOAR's addition takes

---

[23] https://securityintelligence.com/posts/design-thinking-for-privileged-access-management/

into account this newer trend of leveraging automation due to resource constraints and the speed at which events can turn into breaches. Note that PAM has its own SOAR that also sends events to the SOC (Security Operations Center) SOAR.

The IAM and PAM spaces and interactions are better represented in this architecture as well. Importantly, it recognizes that users come from the same direction, whether they are users, auditors, administrators, or approvers. Based on how they are authenticated and authorized in the Organization Identity Store, they are then analyzed in Identity Analytics to determine the level of access they deserve via Cross Identity Management. The level of detail with Endpoints Management, DevOps, Privileged Session Management, and Applications/service accounts aligns better with what we discuss in this book and reflects most organizational realities.

PAM Life Cycle Management

Privileged Access Management requires a life cycle to ensure that these elevated accounts are governed and managed correctly, minimizing the risk to the organization. The main purpose of this book is to demonstrate that this is not a "one and done" task: assign privileged access to the account, rotate it every 90 days, and consider "mission accomplished." That is called compliance and should not be confused with cybersecurity. Cybersecurity necessitates ongoing due diligence and due care, and the same applies to Privileged Access Management. It is a continuous process that must be documented and mapped for users to better understand.

Many existing life cycles consist of seven steps, and while there is nothing wrong with this, our approach elevates the concept to four main stages:

- Define and Discover
- Onboarding
- Monitor and Audit
- Offboarding

Each of these stages has a logical order and control flow. In Define and Discover, the effort is to define what PAM means at your organization and then find out what meets that definition. This is a significant effort that leads to a decision and action stage: Onboarding. This progresses to the Monitor and Audit stage, where activities occur around those "onboarded" accounts, which are subjected to a continuous monitoring effort. Lastly, as with everything, these accounts must eventually conclude, leading to a final decision and action stage: Offboarding.

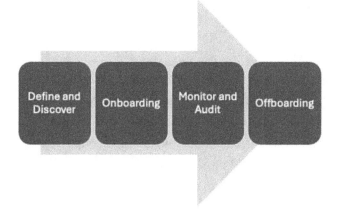

Figure 1-10. *PAM Life Cycle Stages*

Define and Discover

Define what "privileged access" means in your enterprise. We've provided one in this book from the National Institute of Standards and Technology, but it may not be clear enough or specific for your organization. Documenting this in a Privileged Access Management policy or standard is vital. Having this written down ensures everyone in your enterprise is working with the same definition and, therefore, toward the same goal.

In this context, Define also encompasses all the other components of PAM that fall under the Governance category. At the top level, an enterprise should have a cybersecurity policy or standard that mentions privileged access, defines it, and references the appropriate PAM policy/standard document for further details. The Privileged Access Management policy/standard will include definitions for important terminology, designate control points, and reference downstream documents such as runbooks and procedure documents. Once there is an agreed-upon definition of privileged access, the step of Discover involves both identifying which accounts are subject to that definition and assessing their relative risk to the organization. This relative risk ranking allows for a risk-based approach in determining which accounts should advance to the next stage, Onboarding, first.

Onboarding

Onboarding resources into your PAM process requires planning with the end user and security outcomes in mind. As users determine that they need elevated accounts, the process of requesting, approving, and retrieving privileged access tokens must be well mapped out, documented, and auditable. The onboarding process should include control points to ensure that elevated account approvals are appropriately reviewed. Based on both the role and the associated risk, there needs to be approvals for those privileged access requests. For example, if a new payroll clerk needs access to the payroll system to process paychecks, then the clerk must obtain their manager's approval. However, for the person or role that approves the entire company payroll for payment, two approvals are required: both the CFO and the CEO.

Onboarding must consider the items we discussed in lowering the risk to elevated accounts: just-in-time access, MFA, rotating passwords, etc. A workflow should be developed that can be followed by the end users requesting a privileged account. This workflow should highlight the control or decision points, clarify which roles perform each step, and allow for a service turnaround time. Ideally, this onboarding process will be automated to reduce the chances of transpositional error and speed up the time to completion.

Monitor and Audit (Attestation)

Monitoring and auditing is an ongoing process focusing on the six W's: who, what, where, when, why, and how elevated accounts are utilized. Similar to the implementation step of Monitor and Audit, this phase aims to have personnel and tools overseeing access rights. When a role meets the definition of privileged access, it is managed according to the governance model. Audit or attestation occurs regularly (with elevated accounts, this should be done at least quarterly for best practice) to review users' roles and access, determining if it is still necessary. This step reduces the risk of "privilege creep": as users' jobs and roles evolve over time, if that access is not reviewed and adjusted appropriately, their rights may increase gradually or "creep."

Offboarding

Offboarding, like the onboarding process, should be documented so that users understand how to request it or why it has occurred (their PAM account being offboarded). Too often, this aspect is overlooked because it is assumed to be completed as part of the Monitor and Audit stage. However, there are specific steps for how to identify and mitigate risk for a privileged account that is no longer needed, thus making it eligible for offboarding.

Offboarding is an area of PAM that is often neglected due to several factors. First is the issue of "rights creep," where users are never stripped of access rights they no longer need. When a domain administrator is no longer going to perform those duties, their rights must be removed; however, many organizations miss this opportunity and "tack on" the user's new role permissions on top of the domain administrator's rights. Second, many organizations don't distinguish between privileged and ordinary accounts, often elevating users' regular accounts to privileged access.

As indicated earlier, users must have their rights reviewed regularly, which is even more crucial for elevated accounts. This review would reduce the chance of privileged accounts remaining active longer than necessary and ensure no chance of privilege creep occurs.

The Magnificent Seven: PAM Best Practices

As mentioned earlier, Privileged Access Management (PAM) is not a tool or technology but a combination of people, process, and technology. Some key activities and principles ensure success with PAM, and we've compiled the Magnificent Seven PAM Best Practices.

Require MFA

Multifactor authentication (MFA) requires more than one factor to confirm identity at login or at intervals during access. Four factors are available: what you know, who you are, where you are, and what you have. What you know typically refers to a username and password. Username and password are not multifactor; they constitute single-factor authentication. This is a common mistake among cyber novices. Who you are involves biometrics, such as fingerprints or retina scans. Where you are provides a way to geolocate a person and ensure they are in the appropriate location; for example, if you're US-based, and the system detects you logging in from India, it is highly likely that it is not you. What you have involves tokens where a random number generator provides the second factor of authentication.

MFA must be mandated for any elevated account, full stop. This is why it is the first of the Magnificent 7. The authors believe that MFA would be ideal for all users, given the statistics surrounding malicious actors gaining access to accounts through social engineering and phishing attacks. However, that may be a step too far for some organizations, so it must be required for any account with privileged access.

Cross-Platform Support

While most of the world runs on Windows, privileged access is not confined to Windows systems; most enterprises operate multiple platforms. It is crucial to have PAM rolled out across all platforms. It is not expected to implement cross-platform on day 1 of work, but there must be a plan to integrate all systems into your PAM process, people, and technology. Linux, Unix, Windows, Mainframe, and proprietary OS should all have methods to incorporate into your process and technologies surrounding Privileged Access Management.

Temporary Elevated Access (TEA)/JIT

This is often referred to as just-in-time access, but that creates a terrible acronym, and no one wants to write just-in-time access when TEA will suffice. The principle is to ensure resources are accessed only by elevated users or systems when needed. Much like least-privileged access, where only the necessary level of access required for the user to complete their duties is granted, nothing more, TEA further refines access to a duration that minimizes risk. Elevated access should always be granted for a limited time, and the guideline would be to reduce the duration of access based on the risk associated with the resource being accessed. For example, a database containing customer credit cards might allow access for only four hours at a time before a new token is required; a database with partner information (not considered Restricted) would permit access for six to eight hours.

Separation of Duties

Separating duties is a core principle of cybersecurity, and in PAM, it is the best practice for success. An example of this separation in practice is to ensure that all reviews, approvals, and renewals of elevated access rights are conducted by someone other than those requesting them and at a level appropriate for the access risk. This separation includes a review of access rights, ensuring that data owners regularly review who has elevated access to verify that those rights are still needed.

Role-Based Access Control

Role-based access control (RBAC) is crucial for the success of PAM as it is one side of the least-privileged access coin. This type of access provides permissions based on a job or function. In this environment, the enterprise has clearly defined roles with granular rights that are specific to allow individuals or services to perform their designated tasks. The RBAC process defines specific rights and abilities for each role and ensures that users and service accounts with elevated privileges have only those particular rights and skills necessary to fulfill their responsibilities.

Automate

Automation is critical to long-term success for PAM deployments. A few steps in any PAM process, involving people and technologies, can result in missed steps or delays when automation is absent. Initial automation may stretch that definition, meaning it may be a "manual" process initiated due to specific steps that are "automated" in terms of their performance. Ideally, as a strategic goal, the intent is to automate the steps and controls so that they are electronically started at each control point or action step. Automation is a crucial best practice because it is the only way to ensure that the process, people, and technology do not overlook the PAM processes required by policy and procedure.

Maintain and Monitor

Once fully implemented on a system, OS, or whole enterprise, PAM is not complete. Like any system at risk, it requires ongoing care and support. Maintenance involves ensuring the basics (such as software updates, policy updates, reporting, and escalations as appropriate) are fulfilled but also includes more advanced efforts, where enhancing risk reduction or improving efficiencies must be integral to the ongoing process.

Most enterprises don't monitor sufficiently, and Zero Trust requires organizations to enhance their monitoring efforts. Because PAM processes, people, and technologies are at greater risk, they must have improved monitoring and logging for better visibility and transparency.

Zero Trust and PAM Intersection

Privileged Access Management and Zero Trust have a considerable overlap, and that's why this book was written. The three core principles of zero trust are least-privileged access, all resources are accessed securely, and all traffic is monitored. These principles overlap the core principles in PAM best practices. Least privilege is a core concept in both strategies to ensure resources are accessed by only those who need to and the level of access required to perform their role. Accessing resources securely and monitoring all traffic is necessary for Zero Trust and PAM to succeed. Lastly, identity is and always has been the perimeter, so ensuring elevated accounts are secured and used correctly is central to Zero Trust success. The term "Identity is the new perimeter" refers to how, in the old model (M&Ms), the perimeter was the ingress and egress points for the network; in this new model, users access resources in all different ways, and their perimeter, or boundary, is defined by their identity, not their location about the firewall. Zero Trust has many moving parts to be successful, but getting privileged users managed adequately is the long pole in your tent for a successful outcome in any Zero Trust strategy.

The technical reviewer of this book, Jerry Chapman, in his coauthored book *Zero Trust Security*[24] (with Jason Garbis), shares his take on the intersection of Zero Trust and PAM:

> *"Keep in mind that while PAM functions (vaulting, secrets, session recording) will continue to have an important role to play in security architectures, there may be some changes (and potential diminishment) with a Zero Trust environment.*
>
> *As we mentioned previously, many PAM solutions do already have a built-in policy and access model, and are able to integrate with identity providers for user authentication, role-based access control, and attribute-based access control. In this way, there are to some degree acting like policy enforcement points. But let's address the "800-pound gorilla" of PAM – password vaulting. The entire premise of password vaulting is based upon the non-Zero Trust approach for a too-open network, where every user has an ongoing network access to every server, and therefore a vault with server password obfuscation and rotation is required. This premise is no longer trust with Zero Trust! In theory, in a Zero Trust network, you could actually do away with passwords for privileged access to servers, and instead rely on the PEPs to enforce Zero Trust policies, tied to context and business processes. Now we're not suggesting you actually do this, but it is an important perspective, and does illustrate the way in which a Zero Trust network can alter the value proposition of a password vault. We don't recommend actively decommissioning PAM vaults....other functions within PAM – secrets management and session recording – will remain relevant in a Zero Trust world.*

---

[24] Chapman and Garbis, "Zero Trust Security", Apress Publishing, 2021

...The most straightforward and easily achieved approach is to protect access to the PAM server itself, by putting it behind a PEP...In this scenario, the PAM solution is a protected resource within the Zero Trust architecture."[25]

As Jerry and Jason put it in their book, there will be some small impact to PAM with a Zero Trust deployment, but this impact is near negligible in most cases. As we explore Zero Trust in the next chapter, things like a PEP and protected resource will become more familiar.

Chapter Summary

In this chapter, we provided an overview of Privileged Access Management (PAM) to ensure all readers understand this topic as we dive into it more profoundly. We defined a privileged account as "a user that is authorized (and therefore, trusted) to perform security-relevant functions that ordinary users are not authorized to perform."[26] Several types of typical elevated accounts exist, such as service accounts, domain administrators, and application administrators.

The four steps for successful PAM implementation are as follows:

1. Discovery

2. Governance

3. Monitor and Audit

4. Automate

---

[25] "Zero Trust Security: An Enterprise Guide"; Apress Publishing, Jason Garbis, Jerry W. Chapman, 2021

[26] https://csrc.nist.gov/glossary/term/privileged_user

The four steps of a successful PAM life cycle are as follows:

1. Define and Discover

2. Onboarding

3. Monitor and Audit

4. Offboarding

These are the Magnificent Seven PAM Best Practices:

1. Enforce MFA

2. Cross-platform support

3. Temporary elevated access (TEA)

4. Separation of duties

5. Role-based access control (RBAC)

6. Automate

7. Maintain and monitor

Privileged Access Management combines people, processes, and technology to drastically lower the risk of elevated accounts.

CHAPTER 2

Zero Trust: Origins and Evolution

Chapter Overview

In this chapter, we will introduce the concept of Zero Trust, discuss the importance of strategy, provide some history about its origin and development, address principles and misconceptions surrounding Zero Trust, and conclude the chapter with guidelines for successful Zero Trust deployments. The descriptions should not require a cybersecurity certification to understand but a basic grasp of the cybersecurity triad (confidentiality, integrity, and availability) is recommended. The cybersecurity triad (CIA) shapes how cyber professionals assess each risk. Confidentiality involves keeping sensitive data secret or private. Integrity ensures that data is trustworthy and free from unauthorized tampering. Availability means that data, networks, and services must function and be accessible to authorized users. All three of these principles guide cybersecurity teams in addressing risk, and when all three principles are satisfied, the security of an organization improves. As you explore the rest of this book, we will examine Zero Trust and PAM principles, with the CIA triad consistently driving risk identification and mitigation.

© Gregory C. Rasner, Maria C. Rasner 2025
G. C. Rasner and M. C. Rasner, *Privileged Access Management*,
https://doi.org/10.1007/979-8-8688-1431-0_2

Figure 2-1. *CIA Triad*

This is primarily a Privileged Access Management book. Zero Trust is included for two main reasons. First, it is timely, and many organizations that are looking to implement ZT also need to update their PAM programs. Second, the overlap between ZT and PAM is significant enough to warrant the addition. The authors strive to present sufficient information on ZT to assist readers:

- Understand what is Zero Trust

- What Zero Trust is not

- Enable a smoother conversation between the two teams (PAM and ZT)

- Demonstrate there are great resources, consolidated in this book, available for a broader discussion about Zero Trust

This is not a disclaimer, more of an explanation of where the focus is on the book (PAM and how to do it better) and an overlay of how it fits into a Zero Trust strategy.

Zero Trust Overview

What is Zero Trust? There are numerous vendors selling products to help you implement it. Many books have been published about what it is, how to implement it, and how to evolve it in your enterprise. There are a variety of online and in-person classes, seminars, workshops, and forums for Zero Trust. Yet, many organizations struggle with understanding what Zero Trust is (and, more importantly, what it is not).

Zero Trust is a strategy.

That statement is a single sentence to drive home that point: ZT is a strategy designed to lower the risk of an event, incident, or breach. "Zero Trust is a cybersecurity strategy premised on the idea that no user or asset is to be implicitly trusted. It assumes that a breach has already occurred or will occur. Therefore, a user should not be granted access to sensitive information by a single verification done at the enterprise perimeter. Instead, each user, device, application, and transaction must be continually verified."[1]

It is neither a tool nor a technology. A vendor will not solve it for you. A book will not implement it for you. A workshop will not provide you with an "easy button" to smash it into existence in your enterprise. Every organization requires a strategy to set an ultimate goal that drives all tactical decisions (we'll talk about more in the next section). The critical takeaway from this section is that ZT comprises a set of principles, guidelines, and concepts that inform strategic decisions on how to best lower cybersecurity risk. The tools, technologies, instructions, consultants, and other tactical items you enlist are part of that strategy but not Zero Trust itself.

---

[1] https://www.cisa.gov/sites/default/files/publications/NSTAC%20 Report%20to%20the%20President%20on%20Zero%20Trust%20and%20Trusted%20 Identity%20Management.pdf, p. 1

Strategy vs. Tactical

As discussed in the previous section, ZT is a strategy, not a tool or technology. Let's take a few minutes to discuss the importance of strategy and how it can lead to success in Zero Trust and Privileged Access Management. A strategy is a plan of action or policy designed to achieve a primary objective or goal. To put this in perspective, during World War II, there were two opposing sides. The Axis powers consisted of Germany, Italy, and Japan, while the Allies were mainly composed of the United States, the United Kingdom, and the Soviet Union. The strategic goal of the Allies was the complete, unconditional surrender of the Axis powers. All other decisions were aligned with this strategic goal of unconditional surrender. The decisions that contributed to the success of this strategic goal were tactical. Tactical decisions refer to actions or methods used to achieve a strategic goal. In World War II, tactical decisions included the D-Day invasion of Normandy, the Allied invasion of Sicily, and the landings at Iwo Jima and Okinawa. All of these actions aimed to compel Germany, Italy, and Japan to surrender. Having this overall strategy ensured that every decision advanced that goal. This does not imply that some tactics were unsuccessful. Operation Market Garden was a large airborne operation by the Allies in the fall of 1944 aimed at capturing Belgium and the vital port of Antwerp from the Germans. It was a strategic loss and did not meet its objectives, but the operation aligned with the overarching strategy of defeating Germany as a goal.

Figure 2-2. *Plastic WW2*

From a technology and cybersecurity perspective, a strategy is a goal and policy designed to drive your decisions. Zero Trust as a strategy means that all your tactical decisions—what technologies to use, how to implement them, the governance models, and operationalization—are guided by Zero Trust principles. The significance of strategy in cybersecurity and technology ensures that we concentrate on our defined success and do not get sidetracked or misled by technologies or tools that are merely the tactical items we use to achieve strategic success.

Historical Perspectives

Zero Trust was first coined by John Kindervag in 2008 while he was working at Forrester Research. His report, "No More Chewy Centers: Introducing the Zero Trust Model of Information Security," published in September 2010, aimed to pierce the bubble of belief that a perimeter-based, legacy-style firewall network (where the external interface is "untrusted" and the internal interface is "trusted") is the fundamental cause of network and data breaches. In his paper, John used the term "no more chewy centers" and made the comparison of our networks to M&Ms.[2] This analogy illustrates that there is a complex, crunchy exterior, but once past it, there is only delicious, soft chocolate inside. We tend to design and construct our networks and data access similarly, with a crunchy exterior in the form of a firewall, and once inside, the bad actor has free rein of the premises.

Zero trust has become the "vogue" topic in many venues in the more than 14 years since that report was published. The most significant change has come in many organizations that have now adopted frameworks, guidance, training, and testing around Zero Trust. In 2018, the White House established a working group to develop standards around Zero Trust through the Chief Information Office Council and the National Institute of Standards and Technology (NIST).[3] The US government has undertaken several initiatives when it comes to ZT since then, including NIST Special Publication 800-207: Zero Trust Architecture in 2020,[4] an Executive Order (EO 14028): Improving our Nation's Cybersecurity in 2021,[5] and a Federal Zero Trust Strategy in 2022.[6]

In addition, the Cybersecurity and Infrastructure Security Agency (CISA) has taken the lead in providing guidance on Zero Trust. One of the latest and best pieces of advice from CISA comes in their Zero Trust

---

[2] John Kindervag, No More Chewy Centers: Introducing the Zero Trust Model of Information Security, September 14, 2010, Updated September 17, 2010, https://media.paloaltonetworks.com/documents/Forrester-No-More-Chewy-Centers.pdf

[3] Sylvia Burns, Federal Deposit Insurance Corporation, "NSTAC ZT-IdM Subcommittee Briefing," Briefing to the NSTAC Zero Trust and Trusted Identity Management (ZT-IdM) Subcommittee. Arlington, VA, October 13, 2021

[4] NIST, SP 800-207: Zero Trust Architecture, August 2020, https://csrc.nist.gov/publications/detail/sp/800-207/final

[5] EO 14028: Improving the Nation's Cybersecurity, The White House, May 12, 2021, https://www.whitehouse.gov/briefing-room/presidential-actions/2021/05/12/executive-order-on-improving-the-nations-cybersecurity/

[6] Office of Management and Budget, M-22-09: Moving the U.S. Government Toward Zero Trust Cybersecurity Principles, The White House, January 26, 2022, https://www.whitehouse.gov/wp-content/uploads/2022/01/M-22-09.pdf

Maturity Model Version 2.0. Released in April 2023, this 30-page document details Zero Trust, adoption challenges, maturity model by pillar, and some helpful references for the reader. During your Zero Trust journey, checking out CISA's website and publications for additional updates and guidance is always beneficial.

Zero Trust Maturity Journey

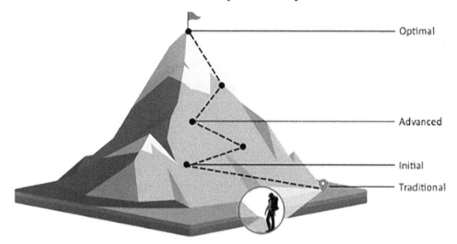

Figure 2: Zero Trust Maturity Journey

Figure 2-3. *CISA ZT Maturity Journey*

Principles and Misconceptions

Let's address the misconceptions first. We've already dispelled some of these: it is not a tool, technology, or hardware. A vendor cannot solve it for you, but they can assist with strategy and tactical goals. Zero Trust has become somewhat of a marketing term rather than a technology security strategy in some areas. The process for implementing Zero Trust is not circular but linear, as it is completed in stages while selecting each "Protect Surface" (more on that later).

Zero Trust encompasses three main concepts: least-privileged access, secure access to all resources, and traffic monitoring. Least-privileged access refers to the idea that a user's ability to connect and interact with resources is limited by their need to know and permitted only. Instead of granting users administrator or super-user privileges, access rights are fine-tuned to allow only the permissions necessary to perform their job. Secure access to resources requires that all traffic be encrypted, regardless of location. Too often, especially on internal networks, unencrypted traffic is permitted, leading to data leakage. Lastly, the concept of monitoring and logging all traffic challenges the old M&M method mentioned by Mr. Kindervag. Rather than simply monitoring and logging traffic at the firewall, active and continual monitoring and logging should also occur within your network.

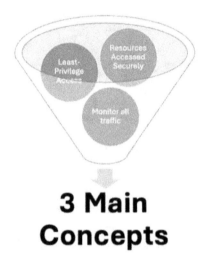

Figure 2-4. *Three Main ZT Concepts*

The reference to M&Ms and a crunchy exterior highlights how networks were traditionally built and perceived: external and internal interfaces on firewalls had labels of "untrusted" and "trusted," respectively, indicating that anything external was untrusted and anything internal was automatically trusted. The premise is that we are too trusting. This perspective led to a focus on monitoring and logging all activity around the firewall (the point of entry and exit); once a user or resource passed through the firewall, they were considered trusted and could essentially perform any action allowed for other trusted resources.

Network administrators and security professionals focused their attention on building (figuratively) bigger and brighter firewalls, along with enhanced defenses and offenses staged at the exterior of the firewall to protect the "trusted" side of the network. This overtrusting nature of the approach led to breach after breach for several reasons, primarily because it is a mistake to assume that just because a resource or user is on your side of the wall, they can be trusted.

This leads to the premise and saying in Zero Trust: "Never Trust, Always Verify." This contrasts with an often-used term in cyber or risk management, "Trust but Verify." This latter saying is derived from a Russian proverb that US President Ronald Reagan employed in negotiations with the Soviets regarding nuclear arms control in the 1980s. Zero Trust asserts that you never trust but consistently verify users and resources to ensure they are who they claim to be and access only the information they have permission to access.

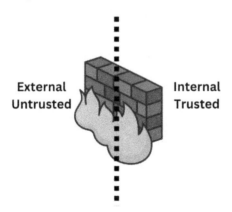

Figure 2-5. *Trusted vs. Untrusted*

There are five steps to deploying Zero Trust. First is defining the Protect Surface. The Protect Surface is crucial in Zero Trust. It is where critical data, assets, applications, and services (DAAS) reside. Not all risks are created equal, allowing your teams to focus on what is truly risky (where your sensitive, critical DAAS resides) and let your Intranet, for example, be "expendable" in the event of an attack. CISA and their publication "Defining the Zero Trust Protect Surface" provide excellent guidance for your enterprise in this exercise concerning Protect Surface decisions and ZT implementation.

Figure 2-6. *ZT Five Implementation Steps*

The second step to deploying ZT is to "Map the transaction flows." In this step, the team works to understand how data traffic moves in and around the protected surface and how the DAAS components interact with network resources. Mapping these traffic flows allows cyber practitioners to identify where to place controls and monitoring around the protected surface and internally for a successful Zero Trust deployment.

The third step is to design a Zero Trust architecture that reflects the outcomes of step 1 (Protect Surface) and step 2 (Map Transaction Flows). This may involve collaboration among security architecture, enterprise architecture, and network architecture teams. These teams review the results of the first two steps and determine how to structure the infrastructure and flow around the protected surface. As a general guideline, controls should be placed as close to the protected surface as possible.

The fourth step is to create a Zero Trust policy. Zero Trust is implemented at layer 7 (Application) and uses policy statements to control access and movement. CISA recommends using the Kiplinger Method—the five W's (who, what, when, where, and why)—to determine who can access DAAS items on the protected surface and when.

The last step, number five, is to monitor and maintain the network. This involves logging and monitoring all traffic up to layer 7. Notice the word use of "all" traffic and not "important" or "some." You cannot make informed decisions if you are not logging all traffic. You're making uninformed decisions, actually. This may involve a severe uplift of your enterprise logging and monitoring capabilities, but Zero Trust will also challenge your resources in other areas (PAM and IAM in particular). Coordinating and correlating all this logging data allows for a contextual understanding of resources and traffic, providing valuable security insights.

These five steps are intended to be executed in a linear fashion as you identify each Protect Surface and/or area of Zero Trust focus in your enterprise. Upon completing one set of Protect Surfaces or areas, the next Protect Surface will be defined, transactions mapped, architecture developed, policies outlined, and monitoring enabled. Rinse and repeat.

Attack Surface vs. Protect Surface: There are often questions about the difference between these similar terms. NIST defines an Attack Surface as "The set of points on the boundary of a system, a system element, or an environment where an attacker can try to enter, cause an effect on, or extract data from, that system, system element, or environment."[7] The Protect Surface generally has a defined boundary since teams have to identify the specific DAAS elements at risk. The Attack Surface constantly moves and changes because of how networks, modern hardware, and software operate. That is the main difference: Protect Surface is a stable environment and does not change, whereas an Attack Surface is in near constant motion due to new vulnerabilities and attack vectors.

---

[7] "Defining the Zero Trust Protect Surface", Cloud Security Alliance, 2024, p. 25

Global Perspectives

Zero Trust guidance and work in the United States are primarily directed by CISA and NIST. However, outside the United States, several other international organizations will guide how ZT is successfully implemented. The National Cyber Security Centre (United Kingdom) has issued recommendations that network architects adopt a Zero Trust approach to deploying new IT infrastructure, emphasizing the importance of cloud deployment. There are specific details for remote access and network architectures available on the NCSC site for Zero Trust deployments. Currently, there is limited EU guidance on Zero Trust implementations. Nonetheless, any efforts in Europe must navigate several regulations, most notably the General Data Protection Regulation (GDPR) and how ZT implementation will comply with GDPR. The other regulatory guidance in the EU:

- EU Cloud of Conduct (EU CoC): Designed to harmonize the GDPR goals across the Cloud Service Providers.

- Trusted Information Security Assessment Exchange (TISAX): Provides industry-specific guidance and framework for assessing information security.

- Digital Operation Resilience Act (DORA): This regulatory framework focuses on IT operational resilience to ensure that organizations are prepared and ready for inevitable disruptions.

At this time, there are no available resources from other regions, apart from the United States, United Kingdom, and EU, on Zero Trust regulatory, architectural, or framework guidance. The guidance would always be to ensure that as you develop a Zero Trust and Privileged Access Management strategy, you consult with appropriate resources for your regulatory oversight and organizational strategic goals.

It All Comes Back to NIST and CISA…and DoD

Now that we've discussed the few international standards that could be viewed as having some Zero Trust guidance, we see that most organizations are leaning into the recommendations from the National Institute of Standards and Technology (NIST), the Cybersecurity and Infrastructure Security Agency (CISA), and, in some cases, the US Department of Defense. We've leveraged the NIST guidance extensively in this book for both the Zero Trust and Privileged Access Management sections. While the localized rules for those outside the United States shouldn't be ignored—because you're likely to run afoul of the supervisory and regulatory agencies managing issues like DORA and TISAX—it is perfectly reasonable for those outside the United States to look to NIST and CISA for guidance on Zero Trust.

CISA's guidance primarily focuses on adoption and how-to guides, which are extremely valuable for practitioners and leaders. In particular, they provide an excellent guide on measuring the maturity of a Zero Trust program. This can be especially challenging since Zero Trust is typically implemented in bursts that concentrate on specific targets. In April 2023, CISA published version 2.0 of the Zero Trust Maturity Model,[8] which offers guidance on measuring your organization's progress in this area.

---

[8]https://www.cisa.gov/sites/default/files/2023-04/zero_trust_maturity_model_v2_508.pdf

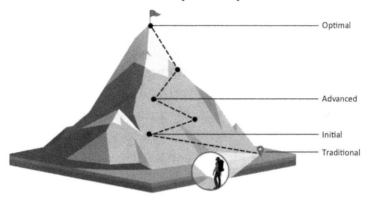

Figure 2-7. *CISA ZT Maturity Journey*

This publication starts with an explanation of what is Zero Trust, Zero Trust architecture, and challenges to the adoption. Then, it gets into the maturity measuring parts and does this by breaking down Zero Trust into five pillars:

- Identity

- Devices

- Networks

- Applications and workloads

- Data

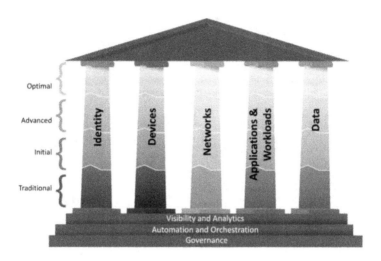

Figure 2-8. *CISA ZT Maturity Evolution*

Underneath these pillars for Zero Trust are the foundations:

- Visibility and Analytics: Visibility refers to the artifacts that must be observable within the enterprise, and analytics is the ability to do scrutiny of this data to make decisions about access or an incident, for example.

- Automation and Orchestration: Automation and orchestration of tools and workflows is the aim of any Zero Trust deployment maturity drivers.

- Governance: Literally the way the entire system, end-to-end, is "governed" or how are the policies, procedures, and processes ensured they are followed and enforced.

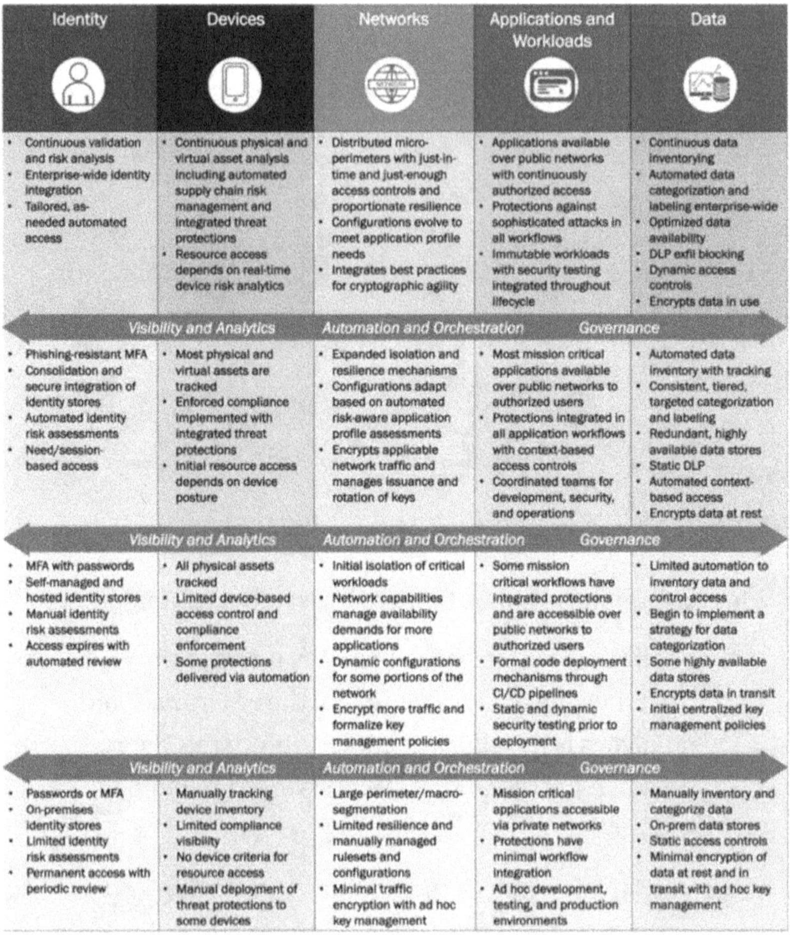

	Identity	Devices	Networks	Applications and Workloads	Data
Optimal	• Continuous validation and risk analysis • Enterprise-wide identity integration • Tailored, as-needed automated access	• Continuous physical and virtual asset analysis including automated supply chain risk management and integrated threat protections • Resource access depends on real-time device risk analytics	• Distributed micro-perimeters with just-in-time and just-enough access controls and proportionate resilience • Configurations evolve to meet application profile needs • Integrates best practices for cryptographic agility	• Applications available over public networks with continuously authorized access • Protections against sophisticated attacks in all workflows • Immutable workloads with security testing integrated throughout lifecycle	• Continuous data inventorying • Automated data categorization and labeling enterprise-wide • Optimized data availability • DLP exfil blocking • Dynamic access controls • Encrypts data in use
	Visibility and Analytics		Automation and Orchestration		Governance
Advanced	• Phishing-resistant MFA • Consolidation and secure integration of identity stores • Automated identity risk assessments • Need/session-based access	• Most physical and virtual assets are tracked • Enforced compliance implemented with integrated threat protections • Initial resource access depends on device posture	• Expanded isolation and resilience mechanisms • Configurations adapt based on automated risk-aware application profile assessments • Encrypts applicable network traffic and manages issuance and rotation of keys	• Most mission critical applications available over public networks to authorized users • Protections integrated in all application workflows with context-based access controls • Coordinated teams for development, security, and operations	• Automated data inventory with tracking • Consistent, tiered, targeted categorization and labeling • Redundant, highly available data stores • Static DLP • Automated context-based access • Encrypts data at rest
	Visibility and Analytics		Automation and Orchestration		Governance
Initial	• MFA with passwords • Self-managed and hosted identity stores • Manual identity risk assessments • Access expires with automated review	• All physical assets tracked • Limited device-based access control and compliance enforcement • Some protections delivered via automation	• Initial isolation of critical workloads • Network capabilities manage availability demands for more applications • Dynamic configurations for some portions of the network • Encrypt more traffic and formalize key management policies	• Some mission critical workflows have integrated protections and are accessible over public networks to authorized users • Formal code deployment mechanisms through CI/CD pipelines • Static and dynamic security testing prior to deployment	• Limited automation to inventory data and control access • Begin to implement a strategy for data categorization • Some highly available data stores • Encrypts data in transit • Initial centralized key management policies
	Visibility and Analytics		Automation and Orchestration		Governance
Traditional	• Passwords or MFA • On-premises identity stores • Limited identity risk assessments • Permanent access with periodic review	• Manually tracking device inventory • Limited compliance visibility • No device criteria for resource access • Manual deployment of threat protections to some devices	• Large perimeter/macro-segmentation • Limited resilience and manually managed rulesets and configurations • Minimal traffic encryption with ad hoc key management	• Mission critical applications accessible via private networks • Protections have minimal workflow integration • Ad hoc development, testing, and production environments	• Manually inventory and categorize data • On-prem data stores • Static access controls • Minimal encryption of data at rest and in transit with ad hoc key management

Figure 2-9. *High-Level Zero Trust Maturity Model Overview*

The agency then breaks down the maturity into four levels:

- Traditional: This is the "base" of the maturity model, and, as one would expect, it is a world in which everything is manual. Many of the items required for Zero Trust to be successful are accomplished with only manual intervention and pushing. There is very little, if any, real-time visibility on systems.

- Initial: Automation is beginning to occur in the Zero Trust model, with certain attributes, enforcement mechanisms, and solutions featuring varying levels of automation at several control points. There is some visibility into internal systems.

- Advanced: Automated controls are established for the life cycle, ensuring effective cross-pillar coordination and integration. There is centralized visibility that allows insight beyond internal solutions to externally hosted resources.

- Optimal: Fully automated, all subject and resource interaction is automated and orchestrated, with dynamic policies firing off like unicorns belching up rainbows. It's kind of a dream spot where everyone strives to achieve, but few will succeed given some of the legacy issues that many larger enterprises still face in production.

Zero Trust Architecture

The National Institute of Standards and Technology has published Special Publication 800-207 Zero Trust Architecture.[9] The documentation allows that there are potentially "several ways that an enterprise can enact a ZTA (Zero Trust Architecture) for workflows."[10] All of the different approaches include Zero Trust principles and enhanced identity governance-driven, micro-segmentation, and network segmentation. The document then dives into the different approaches to enable different ZT solutions.

---

[9] https://nvlpubs.nist.gov/nistpubs/SpecialPublications/NIST.SP.800-207.pdf

[10] https://nvlpubs.nist.gov/nistpubs/SpecialPublications/NIST.SP.800-207.pdf, p. 11

Enhanced Identity Governance ZTA

In this architectural approach, as the name implies, the identity of the subject is the key factor in policy creation for ZT. Each subject is required to have access privileges to connect to a resource. Although access to a resource is primarily based on the identity characteristics of the subject, this does not mean that other attributes, such as the type of device used, device health, and other policy factors, are excluded from consideration; they are simply not the primary focus. Enterprise resource access policies prioritize identity and attributes in policy creation. This approach is most effective in scenarios with an open network that permits initial connectivity by visitors and frequent nonorganizational devices. Additionally, this architecture is well-suited for instances where an organization utilizes many cloud-based applications in a complex hybrid environment. In such cases, a centralized resource portal should be used to provide access decisions regarding device identity and policy information for initial connectivity.

In a Zero Trust strategy, it is reasonable to assert that this model is the best option for success. As you create a policy, it should consider these four items: principle, action, resource, and condition. These four elements define the permissions granted to an entity for access (user or role). They work to determine who can do what to which resources and under what conditions. The principal is the entity that the policy applies to, action refers to the actions the principal can take, resource is the actual "thing" being accessed, and condition allows for more specific control over when the policy applies (such as IP addresses, time, etc.).

Micro-segmentation ZTA

This architecture relies on a gateway security component, such as a next-generation firewall (NGFW), intelligent routers or switches, or another device used as a special-purpose gateway. Another implementation of this architecture can be seen when an organization uses software agents to enact host-based micro-segmentation. This type of gateway allows subjects to connect to resources dynamically. This model enables the gateway to serve as a sole Policy Enforcement Point or as part of a multipart PEP that incorporates both the gateway and the client agent for segmentation.

In this architecture, there are several methods for deployment, including leveraging the PEP to function as the protecting device, while the management of the devices is handled by the Policy Engine and Policy Administrator. NIST indicates that this method requires your identity governance program to be very mature (they use the term "fully function") to allow the gateway components to enable the PEP to act as a shield to resources in a ZT architecture.

Network Infra and SDP ZTA

As the name indicates, this architecture of ZT leverages the network infrastructure to implement Zero Trust architecture. The implementation of Zero Trust Architecture would be performed using the network overlay, from layer 7 in the OSI model or lower in the stack. This approach is sometimes called Software Defined Perimeter (SDP) and includes elements from Software Defined Networks (SDN). In an SDN deployment, there will be an SDN Controller (SDNC) that pushes the policies to the agents and gateway for access controls. In this architectural approach, the Policy Administrator will become the network controller that designs and (re)configures the network and devices based on the decisions from the Policy Engine. The subjects will make requests to the Policy Enforcement Points, which are managed by the PA. This method is often implemented at layer 7 in the OSI model (application layer), and the Policy Enforcement Point establishes an encrypted communications channel with the subject and resource.

More About Software Defined Networks

The National Security Agency has published a document that explains what SDNs are and their advantages. It is titled "Managing Risk from SDN Controllers"[11] and outlines the issues and solutions in straightforward business language, making it accessible to most readers. Software Defined Networking (SDN) enables networks to be centrally managed through a management server known as an SDN Controller (SDNC). The SDNC is configured by administrators with policies to align with the organization's enterprise network micro-segmentation requirements. As these policies are set on the SDNC, they are "pushed" to network devices for operational implementation. The SDNC also governs switch and router traffic for enterprise network communications.

This centrally managed system stands in contrast to the traditional method of updating network devices (switches, routers, firewalls). This older method (before SDN and the use of SDNC) required the administrator to log into each individual device to configure policies. In this Software Defined Network, the administrator only needs to log into the SDN Controller to make changes to traffic routing. The SDNC should be capable of detecting changes in the enterprise network to enable it to update the mapping and alter device configuration and routing options based on those changes.

The biggest risk in using or leveraging an SDN-based solution for Zero Trust Architecture is the SDN Controller. Because of the power this system holds—as the controller for all Software Defined Networking—it requires better protection. For a Zero Trust deployment, this means ensuring that you make the SDN Controller one of the devices surrounded by extra security. The NSA recommends leveraging a Privileged Access Workstation (often called a jump-box) that is the only allowed system to connect to the SDN Controller and can be used only locally. If remote access is required for the SDN Controller, it should be restricted to a dedicated management network. Lastly, the NSA recommends that organizations allow access to the management

---

[11] https://media.defense.gov/2023/Dec/12/2003357491/-1/-1/0/CSI_
MANAGING_RISK_FROM_SDN_CONTROLLERS.PDF

interface of the SDN Controller only from the dedicated PAW, which restricts non-SDN activities (such as email, web browsing, and office applications). There are more recommendations in the document, and it is not a long read, so you should definitely add it to your library of reference material.

Deployment Options for ZTA

There are several options for deploying this architecture, which can be viewed as simple. It is simple for a reason: to allow for ease of use and application. It is expected that most enterprises will have components in that network that perform multiple functions or tasks within the ZT architecture. For example, an organization's cryptographic PKI server will have multiple roles within the network: certificates for devices, certificates for resources, and certificates for users or subjects.

Device Agent/Gateway-Based Deployment

This deployment model will have the PEP separated into two components that sit on the resources or in front of the resource. One example is that each asset in the enterprise will have an installed agent that coordinates the connections to subjects and resources. When it is placed in front of the resource, it acts much like a proxy. This agent ensures that the resources only communicate directly with the gateway securely. The gateway facilitates communication between the PA and ensures that only approved networking paths are configured.

This type of deployment works best in organizations with a mature and robust device management program, which is essential for success. This model does not support Bring Your Own Device (BYOD) implementations, as it requires a device agent to be installed on resources for effectiveness. In most cases, only enterprise-owned devices or resources can have this agent installed.

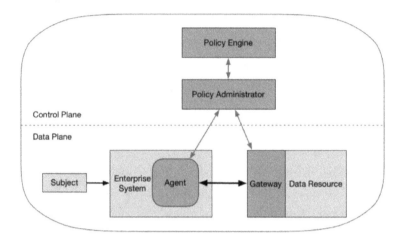

Figure 2-10. *Device/Agent Model*

This deployment scenario typically involves an enterprise-issued desktop or laptop that connects to an enterprise resource. For example, the HR director logs into their laptop and wants to connect to the HR database to perform their job functions. The request for access is processed by the software agent running on the laptop and forwarded to the Policy Administrator. The PA and PE can be on-premises or cloud-based. When the request is authorized, the Policy Administrator establishes a secure communications connection between the device (HR laptop) and the resource gateway via the Control Plane. The PA will then terminate the connection when the work is completed or if a security event requires action by the PA.

Enclave-Based Deployment

The enclave-based deployment takes a variation of the device agent/ gateway-based deployment. Unlike in the above reference model, the agents does not run on the resources or in front of the resources; instead, they reside at the boundary of the resource enclave (think of a DMZ type environment). This model for deployment is best for organizations that leverage cloud-based services that they use for a critical service and also for enterprises with legacy applications (that are difficult or impossible to make ZT-compatible) or on-premises data centers that are not conducive to having individual gateways.

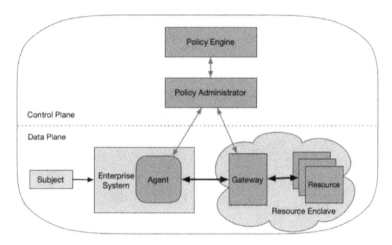

Figure 2-11. *Enclave Gateway Model*

In this model, it is critically important for the organization to have a strong and mature asset and configuration management governance program in place. The downside with this deployment model is that it relies on a single gateway for access to multiple resources, causing a single point of failure risk or the overexposure to assets the subject shouldn't have access to in the policies. This model can be deployed in a hybrid model with the previous Device/Agent approach, with enterprise resources having an agent that connects to the enclave gateway.

Resource Portal-Based Deployment

This deployment model requires a Policy Enforcement Point to function as a single unit performing the gateway function for subject access requests. The gateway portal can be used for an individual resource or leveraged on an enclave gateway for access to multiple resources. The figure below illustrates this model with a gateway portal into a data center or cloud that utilizes legacy applications.

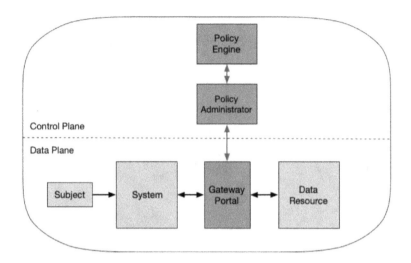

Figure 2-12. *Resource Portal Model*

In this model, there are no local agents that handle access and communication requests. This results in the organization's enterprise not necessarily having a full view or control over the resources all the time but only when they connect to the portal. There are ways to deal with this risk by leveraging browser isolation. This approach is also known as remote browsing, which reduces the risk of webpage content executing malicious code. Typically, a visitor to a website receives the content and code loaded directly into their local browser. In remote browsing mode, the page loads and executes in the cloud, away from the local device.

Architecture Value and Patterns

As we discuss architecture, much of the conversation and documentation is done in a very general method. Time and again, the authors will use terms such as "individual results may vary" or similar when providing these architecture examples. The value of architecture is to design a high-level structure and organization of a system to outline the foundational components, how they interact, and how the system flows end-to-end.

Much like an architect designs the high-level features of a building, the architecture in ZT focuses on the macro-level parts of the system and how implementation would work at the top level. Adopting these architectures allows the teams that implement the technologies and processes to determine how to do that within the parameters laid out by the architecture.

The next step, once an architecture is developed for Zero Trust in your enterprise, is to use it as a pattern. As we mentioned, the architectures presented are all designed to serve as examples, allowing organizations to determine which best fits their organizational reality, strategy, and capabilities. Develop the architecture so that it can be used as a pattern for reuse as new Zero Trust solutions become necessary. Consider how the architecture can be best utilized multiple times instead of being a one-time solution.

Zero Trust Architecture Implementation

Zero Trust Architecture (ZTA) implementation is discussed in depth by the National Institute of Standards and Technology (NIST) in Special Publication 1800-35, "Implementing a Zero Trust Architecture Project," which had its latest publication in July 2024. A Zero Trust architecture is designed to enable secure authorized access to resources, whether they are on-premises or in the cloud and whether the users are on-site or in far remote locations. The NIST 1800-35 is the "NIST Cybersecurity Practice Guide," which takes concepts and principles from the National Institute of Standards and Technology Special Publication 800-207, Zero Trust Architecture. The guide maps out ZTA principles to commonly used security standards and guidance.

Figure 2-13 presents a high-level logical architecture for Zero Trust design. Much like any drawn architecture, this is intended to be general and for reference, not specific to how to deploy detailed resource or user controls. At the bottom of the figure, there are two important components: subject and resource. A subject refers to a user, application, or device that operates on or within an IT system and requests access to a resource. The resource may be data, an application, a workload, or even a document. There are three main types of core components in a Zero Trust architecture: Policy Engines (PE), Policy Administrators (PA), and Policy Enforcement Points (PEP). Policy Engines are the core of the architecture and determine whether to grant access to a resource on the network. Policy Administrators create or halt communication based on the decisions from the Policy Engine. Both the Policy Engine and Policy Administrator constitute the Policy Decision Point (PDP). The PDP is the mechanism through which the PE and PA evaluate resource access requests. Policy Enforcement Points are the systems responsible for enabling, monitoring, and stopping connections between the subject and the resource.

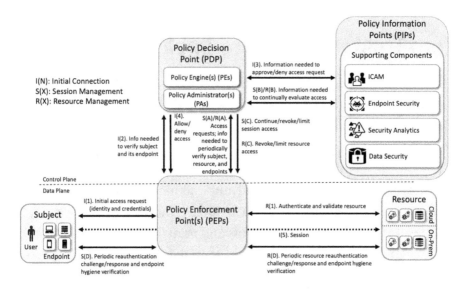

Figure 2-13. *ZTA*

Let's clarify what is meant by the Resource Management and Session steps depicted in the figure. Resource management processes are carried out to ensure that the resource is authenticated on the network and confirmed to adhere to the enterprise network policies for network access. This policy check verifies that the resource is accurate and up-to-date with patches and protocols necessary for accessing the enterprise network—this constitutes a "health" check. Once the health check is completed, the resource is permitted to connect to the Policy Enforcement Point (PEP). This connection to the PEP then enables the Policy Decision Point (PDP) to grant access to the resource based on the rules established in the access policies. Furthermore, the resource is periodically and continuously reauthenticated to ensure compliance with health and policy requirements.

Session Initiation Steps are the sequence of activities that conclude with the establishment of the initial session with the subject and the resources. These steps all occur in sequential order (as described in further detail below). Session Management Steps are the sequence of activities that allow the Policy Decision Point (PDP) to continuously assess the connection between the subject and the resource to ensure adherence to policy. NIST does explain that the steps S(A) through S(D) are not meant to imply an ordering, as the S(1) to S(5) do in Session Initiation Steps.

On the upper right, the architecture describes the Policy Information Points (PIP). This box contains several systems: Identity, Credential and Access Management (ICAM), Endpoint Detection and Response (EDR), Security Analytics, and Data Security Systems. The PIP is in contact with the Policy Decision Point (PDP) to receive information from the PDP to evaluate whether the subjects can access the resources on the network. This is represented by the Initial Connection and Session Management connectivity between the two boxes (PDP and PIP). Both the PDP and PIP are within the Control Plane.

Identity, Credential, and Access Management (ICAM) is a term used by NIST and CISA to describe the domain that encompasses what we typically consider Identity and Access Management (IAM), along with the relevant systems for performing authentication and authorization. When you see the term ICAM, think of IAM with more of that domain included. Endpoint Detection and Response is an integrated, multilayered approach to managing the physical devices that connect to the network, featuring continuous monitoring and rule-based automated responses. Security Analytics employs various tools to assist in identifying, protecting, and troubleshooting security events on the network by utilizing both real-time and logged historical data. Data Security Systems refer to the systems and processes established to protect digital information throughout its entire life cycle from theft, unauthorized access, or alteration.

Under the Control Plane, the Data Plane contains the Policy Enforcement Points (PEP). As the Policy Decision Point and Policy Information Points interact to determine whether the subject can access the resource based on the policies, this information is passed to the PEP. The PEP is responsible for receiving authorization requests sent from the PDP for evaluation. NIST defines the PEP simply as "A system entity that requests and subsequently enforces authorization decisions." Note how the Policy Enforcement Point sits between the Subject and the Resource boxes. The initial request from the Subject to the PEP is made with identity and credentials (I(1) initial access request). This information is then passed along to the PDP to verify the data needed to confirm the subject and the endpoint (I(2)); this information is passed to the PIP, where items such as the ICAM and Endpoint Security are engaged (I(3)). Once the access request is approved or denied, it is passed back to the PDP and then to the PEP (I(4)), which will then allow the session to take place between the Subject and Resource (I(5)).

Along with the initial authentication and authorization steps that take place above, there is work being done to continually or periodically reauthenticate the subject and resource connection. There are Session Management and Resource Management flows and processes that are listed in the architecture.

Zero Trust Policy

The basic premise of Zero Trust is that no subject shall have access to a resource without a policy that supports and directs how the subject is able to interact with the resource. This dynamic policy is the bedrock of how Zero Trust works because, without the policy in place, the subject will not be able to connect to the resource. That's Zero Trust: trust is not default but must be given based upon context-aware policies. This section will discuss in detail the items that make up the Zero Trust policy.

Policy Factors

At a high level, there are four basic policy parts in Zero Trust. These four items will provide the necessary context for a PDP to determine if a subject can connect to a resource:

- Subject Criteria: This is the entity requesting the action or connection; lists what subject (user) is allowed to connect to the resource (target).

- Action: The activity the subject is requesting to perform on the resource.

- Target: The resource the action is being asked to do by the subject.

- Condition: The conditions the subject must meet to connect to the resource.

These are the four common policy pieces leveraged in Zero Trust deployments. Some organizations may not list all five individually, but their policies must contain elements of them to be effective.

Subject Criteria

These are the objects initiating the action for connectivity or interaction with the resource. The subjects must be authenticated and authorized to perform the action. The policy itself will not contain the subject name but will include the criteria that the Policy Decision Point will use to determine if the policy applies to the subject initiating the request. Subject criteria can include any contextual information that is relevant: Active Directory (AD) group membership, device status and health, and information regarding who, what, when, where, why, and how about the subject requesting to connect to a resource.

Action

Actions are simply those activities that the subject is permitted to perform on the resource. This action can occur at either the network layer, the application layer, or both. In a network-defined action, it dictates what actions the subject can take to access the resource. For example, here are some sets of network-defined actions:

- Subject to access resource via HTTP via port 80

- Subject to access resource via RDP via port 3389

- Subject to access resource via SMB via port 445

Other actions can be based on application-specific actions. These can include but are not limited to

- Subject to perform Ctrl+Alt+Delete on the Windows server via RDP

- Subject to perform clearing of the application log via SSH

- Subject to initiate a reboot of a system via HTTPS

It isn't always possible for a Zero Trust deployment to take actions at the application level due to limitations on access to that level within most legacy applications. However, as many applications are being migrated (or have already been migrated) to the cloud, there is an ever-increasing number of applications that will permit this level of granularity and control.

Target

Targets are meant to define the resource being accessed. They can be a host, server, system, or component. Targets can be defined both statically and dynamically. Static policies would state "access to host 10.1.1.20," which specifies that the subject will connect to the resource located at 10.1.1.20. That's it; the Policy Enforcement Policy can process this policy on the target faster than any other. Another example is using a specific host name: "access to host appserver.sample.com/internal," which provides a very clear line of communication for connecting. This offers better flexibility than an IP address since those can change but hostnames don't change (as often). Lastly, "access to hosts on subnet 10.1.1.0/18" is static but allows for a broad access pool of potential targets.

While most policies may start out as static, the true power of Zero Trust lies in leveraging dynamic policies for targets. This enables the Zero Trust system to address subjects requesting access to resources that are not known at the time the policy is written. Leveraging these dynamics can be best illustrated by using tags or labels in systems. Using these tags in instances such as "access to systems tagged as 'human resources'," "access to systems tagged as 'VendorName1'," or "access to systems tagged as 'stage=development'" allows for more dynamic decisions to be made by the PEP and harnesses the power of Zero Trust more effectively.

Condition

Condition is the factor that explains the context in which the subject can connect and perform actions with the resource (target). Conditions should be extensive and extensible for Zero Trust to function most effectively. Allowing organizations to have flexible conditions accommodates not only a potentially large number of contexts but also some custom conditions that an organization may want to create. As indicated, there can be dozens of conditions, but we can list some typical ones that most organizations consider:

- Time: What time of day is the subject attempting to access the resource or target? If this is during a nontypical time, a well-tuned system would deny access or require additional verification.

- Location: Are both the subject and target in the same location (on-premises vs. offshore)? Are they in different levels of environment (test vs. production).

- Resource Risk: Does the target tag describe it as a risk that is critical to the organization and requires additional verification of identity and continual checks every 60 minutes?

- Device Health: Does the device that the subject is connecting with have up-to-date antivirus and operating system patches?

This provides the Zero Trust systems with the ability to make context-aware decisions about subjects, resources, and targets. Let's take a look at a simpler way to view the questions to ask when creating Zero Trust policy.

Six Questions ZT Policy Must Ask (5 W's + 1 H)

The explanations of the Zero Trust policy above are standard for readers learning how to formulate policies. However, a more fundamental way to approach it is through the perspective of the English writer Thomas Wilson (1524–1581), who first introduced the concept in medieval writing: who, what, where, when, why, and how. As you develop the policies, considering this context can assist readers in understanding how to implement them:

- **Who**

    This is the first and most basic of the questions: Who can access this resource? Zero trust must implement strong user authentication and robust device identification. Verification should involve biometrics, multifactor authentication, and ensuring that the device they are connecting with is up-to-date and communicates using encryption. Determined by verified and validated user and device identifications, the policy will define which resources a subject can connect with for access. The "who" must have a valid business reason to access the resource.

- **What (Application and Value)**

    What application is being used to access the resource? This is the next question. The Zero Trust policy should identify applications leveraged to access a resource based on layer 7 information. Also being captured and evaluated in the "what" section are items such as port, protocol, and IP addresses used. This level of information makes it much harder for a bad actor to fool a system into allowing access to a resource.

What value does the resource hold is an important contextual question here in policies. Leveraging both data classification and risk classification programs can help determine what level of risk the resource presents to the enterprise. The higher the value, the higher the risk; therefore, the threshold for subject access to the protected resource must be elevated accordingly.

- **When**

The question of timing is very important, and this points to several criteria and decisions regarding when access should be granted. For example, the JIT (just-in-time) or TEA (temporary elevated access) is part of the timing discussion. Privileged accounts, in particular, should not have access on "24/7/365" as that poses an unnecessary and silly risk. Granting a fixed time window for the elevated account owner to perform their tasks is crucial. Additionally, there may be conditions regarding time periods when an action on a resource can occur. For instance, a policy might state that this resource cannot be accessed during business hours for maintenance updates (e.g., performing an administrator activity may require disconnecting all users from the system). This time-bounding of the activity related to the resource addresses a crucial "when" question. Utilizing behavioral analytics in this area is an excellent approach to determine if a subject is attempting to connect with a resource during an "unusual" time frame.

- **Where**

  One area often forgotten in this day is the "where are the subject and resource located?" Simple ways to limit risk in policies concerning geofencing can ensure users or subjects connect only to relevant resources. A US-based organization with no overseas operations or personnel would be wise to implement a condition that prohibits privileged access from offshore to the United States. The criteria for location can be extensive, but here are some examples:

  - Cloud-based resources

  - Third-party resources

  - Automated systems connecting via API

  - Subjects connecting from external networks

  - Subjects connecting from internal networks

  - On-premises resources

  - Offshore subjects

- **Why**

  Why is a shorter question in this context, but it relates to why does the subject need access to the resource, and is that reason valid for the policy? The subjects role, for example, in a role-based access model will determine the why for access.

- **How**

    A Zero Trust policy and its success depend on appropriately regulating (limiting) access for subjects to resources. The question of how access should be granted to these resources is the final consideration and addresses more of the context of connectivity. Some of the questions regarding how this should occur are as follows but not limited to

    - Granular Access: Ensuring that only the level of access that is required by the subject is allowed.

    - Analysis of Payload: By being able to inspect encrypted traffic (with the help of NGFWs placed throughout your enterprise), this will determine if a malicious package is being sent, data is being exfiltrated, or the communications is being used for malicious purposes.

    - DNS Analysis: Analyzing DNS signatures to detect if there is anything suspicious about the domain naming services actions being taken.

Take these six questions as you develop Zero Trust policies, and throw them up against each other to see if there is a match in intent and outcomes. Very often policies developed, when not taken in comparison to this plain-spoken questions, can find they've missed an important criteria in the policies.

Trust Algorithm

Much of the discussion above has concentrated on criteria-based approaches to how Zero Trust decisions are made. NIST allows and directs a score-based approach, necessitating a discussion about how to develop a "trust algorithm" to be as accurate as possible. A score-based criteria system determines a confidence level based on the values of all data sources and the enterprise-wide configured weighting. If the score exceeds the established threshold, access is granted; if not, connectivity from the subject to the resource is denied.

NIST provides some guidance in this space as well.[12] In the NIST SP 800-207, there is a section that discusses the algorithm and how to best process the data. NIST puts it well:

> *For an enterprise with a ZTA deployment, the policy engine can be thought of as the brain and the PE's trust algorithm as its primary thought process. The trust algorithm (TA) is the process used by the policy engine to ultimately grant or deny access to a resource. The policy engine takes input from multiple sources (see Section 3): the policy database with observable information about subjects, subject attributes and roles, historical subject behavior patterns, threat intelligence sources, and other metadata sources.*[13]

NIST goes on to describe items that would go into the algorithm as access request, subject database, asset database, resource requirements, and threat intelligence. These five items line up very closely to the policy factors discussed above (subject criteria, action, target, condition),[14] and the one that is different is threat intelligence, but the author would contend that this is best fed into the condition policy factor. This additional elevates the efficacy of a Zero Trust deployment because if you can feed threat intelligence into that policy decision, the organization is able to get even finer grained context decisions based upon threats identified in real time.

---

[12] https://nvlpubs.nist.gov/nistpubs/SpecialPublications/NIST.SP.800-207.pdf p. 17–20

[13] https://nvlpubs.nist.gov/nistpubs/SpecialPublications/NIST.SP.800-207.pdf, p. 17

[14] "Zero Trust Security: An Enterprise Guide", Chapman and Garbis, Apress Publishing 2021

Keys to Success

Zero Trust is a collaborative effort not confined to cybersecurity teams but will encompass many teams, from IT to the business leadership. Because of this, it is necessary to have some guidelines called "keys to success." Cloud Security Alliance (CSA) provides excellent guidance in an article listing the 11 guiding principles of the Zero Trust security journey.[15] We've boiled these down to three keys to success. Three primary keys to Zero Trust success are planning, scope, and leadership. Notice that none of these are technologies, tools, or tricks.

Zero Trust is a strategy that requires planning. Strategy is never finalized with zero planning or carried out ad hoc. Key activities within the planning include understanding your risk appetite. What level of risk can your organization safely absorb, and what risk must be transferred, mitigated, or avoided? This risk tolerance level should be established at the highest levels of leadership and then quantified more precisely within the lower levels of risk management teams. Planning also involves considering what you expect to accomplish by the end of your Zero Trust journey. What does the conclusion look like, and what will assist your teams in determining the path to completion?

Zero Trust can be challenging, so the planning phase should also focus on simplicity. Simplicity implies that your team starts with small goals first and then looks to expand Zero Trust into other areas of your enterprise. Identify areas where Zero Trust can significantly impact with minimal effort, deploy it on those critical assets, and then learn from this "smaller" effort to tackle more significant challenges. Lastly, planning should involve a professional, such as a project manager, program manager, SCRUM master, or someone similar, who can effectively guide your Zero Trust journey to ensure success. Never underestimate the impact of an exceptional project management professional in achieving project success.

---

[15] https://cloudsecurityalliance.org/blog/2023/09/29/what-are-the-main-concepts-of-zero-trust

Scope presents a significant challenge in any large project or initiative, and Zero Trust projects are no exception. Determine the scope of what will be included in each Zero Trust implementation around each Protect Surface. Part of this effort should also involve listing what is outside the scope. Identifying items that are outside the scope helps eliminate assumptions or confusion regarding what will and will not be accomplished as part of this effort. Scope can additionally encompass training and other elements essential for success.

Lastly, leadership is, in many ways, the most critical factor for success. This key success factor manifests in a couple of ways for Zero Trust. First, the Zero Trust journey and strategy must be endorsed and fully supported by your most senior leadership. ZT can be a significant, multiteam effort; having this leadership support and direction ensures that the teams understand the priority of the effort. Ideally, your team should find an executive sponsor from the Board of Directors or C-suite who can provide that leadership and direction at regular meetings.

Leadership involves cultivating a Zero Trust culture. Zero Trust is a new approach to the old M&M method and requires teams to rethink their perspectives on various issues and activities. ZT is a shared responsibility among many teams in most organizations, often extending beyond technical teams. Ensure your journey includes actions that begin to educate and align with the requirements for a successful Zero Trust culture.

Chapter Summary

Zero Trust is approaching 20 years since it was first coined by John Kindervag, and since then, it has been widely embraced as a critical strategy for reducing cyber risk. Zero Trust is a strategy, not a set of tools or technologies. A vendor does not have an "easy button" to implement it. While some vendors provide excellent tools and technologies as part of your ZT deployment, it is essential to remember that this strategy requires leadership, scope, and planning for successful deployment and ongoing production. Ensure your teams understand vital issues such as the five steps to successful implementation and the three core ZT principles. Lastly, recognize that Zero Trust focuses on people, processes, and programs for success, meaning it represents a culture shift that requires robust support and engagement from senior leadership.

CHAPTER 3

Assessments and Solutions

Chapter Overview

In this chapter, we will discuss:

- Strategy, Again: As we discuss how to assess and tools, it is important to stress strategy as a central theme in decision-making.

- Importance of Frameworks: A short discussion of why frameworks are important to the success of cybersecurity.

- Current State: How does an organization determine their current PAM state so work can be done to resolve gaps identified.

- Assessment and Risk-Based Approach: Taking a risk-based approach is crucial to success as well as having a solid program and project management oversight.

© Gregory C. Rasner, Maria C. Rasner 2025
G. C. Rasner and M. C. Rasner, *Privileged Access Management*,
https://doi.org/10.1007/979-8-8688-1431-0_3

- Zero Trust Journey Assessment: there are some great tools on how to assess a Zero Trust journey that can be leveraged.

- Chapter Summary: Overview of what we've covered and a reminder of what was important.

Strategy, Again

In Chapter 2, under Zero Trust, the concept of strategy was briefly discussed because having one is essential for organizations to stay on track with their Zero Trust and PAM goals. Strategy holds significance here, once again, because as we introduce tools and technologies, it is very easy for organizations and the individuals involved to lose focus on their goals and become captivated by the tools and technologies. In fact, it is not uncommon for teams or individuals to regard a tool or technology as "the solution" or "the program." As mentioned, these are tools and technologies, so consider them as means to achieve success, rather than success in itself.

Let's take another example to demonstrate: imagine you're building battery-powered electric cars called *Nikolai*. *Nikolai* is publicly traded, which means it has a Board of Directors and shareholders to whom someone must answer for financial success. The Grand Strategy of Nikolai is to maximize profits for the shareholders so they can receive a return on their investment.

The strategy of the Nikolai production team is to produce at least 1000 automobiles a day because that is what the finance team has stated they can do to maximize profits per unit sold. Any more sold, and they start to lower productivity due to size constraints at their factory; any less, and their profit per unit is below the maximum at 1,000 per day. Every decision made regarding processes, tools, and technology serves this goal of 1,000 vehicles per day. The manufacturing team will then make decisions about the processes, tools, and technologies they will need to purchase to meet the set production goals. This includes robots, trained personnel, experienced managers, large capital investments involved in large manufacturing operations, and more.

The fancy welding robots and automated pressing machines look very impressive and do a great job, but they do not achieve the strategy in isolation. They are tools to achieve the strategy. Once the goal of manufacturing 1,000 battery-powered vehicles per day is reached, the Grand Strategy for Nikolai—maximizing profits for shareholders—will be realized. As we progress through the chapter, keep your organization's strategy in the forefront of your mind, and resist the temptation to believe that the tools and technologies are the strategy.

Strategy Examples

The authors are hesitant to prescribe a strategy for organizations reading this book. However, we can posit some very common strategies for most cyber organizations. Good examples can be found in publications by US government agencies. We do have a few critiques regarding them, which we will explain as we review them.

A good example is found in the Department of Homeland Security's Cybersecurity Goals. The Department of Homeland Security lists seven (7) DHS Cybersecurity Goals,[1] and they break it down by pillars:

Pillar I: Risk Identification

- Goal 1: Assess Evolving Cybersecurity Risks

  - Understand the evolving national cybersecurity risk posture to inform and prioritize risk management activities.

---

[1]https://www.dhs.gov/sites/default/files/publications/DHS-Cybersecurity-Fact-Sheet.pdf

Pillar II: Vulnerability Reduction

- Goal 2: Protect Federal Government
  Information Systems

  - Reduce the vulnerabilities of federal agencies to
    ensure they achieve an adequate level of cybersecurity.

- Goal 3: Protect Critical Infrastructure

  - Partner with key stakeholders to ensure that national
    cybersecurity risks are adequately managed.

Pillar III: Threat Reduction

- Goal 4: Prevent and Disrupt Use of Cyberspace

  - Reduce cyber threats by countering transnational
    criminal organizations and sophisticated cyber
    criminals.

Pillar IV: Consequence Mitigation

- Goal 5: Respond Effectively to Cyber Incidents

  - Minimize consequences from potentially
    significant cyber incidents through coordinated
    community-wide response efforts.

Pillar V: Enable Cybersecurity Outcomes

- Goal 6: Strengthen the Security and Reliability of the
  Cyber Ecosystem

  - Support policies and activities that enable
    improved global cybersecurity risk management.

- Goal 7: Improve Management of DHS Cybersecurity Activities

  - Execute our departmental cybersecurity efforts in
    an integrated and prioritized way.

This strategy list is good, but it presents challenges. First, the good news is that it has clearly been reviewed, vetted by leadership, and published. Many organizations don't bother to do this much, which affects their success as they wander from issue to issue without a strategy to define an endpoint. The list offers a solid foundation of things to focus on in the coming years, as they indicated this is a multiyear strategy guide.

One of the better examples in the government, this document also demonstrates what "outcomes" (along with objectives and sub-objectives) are expected for each of the goals. Let's demonstrate how they accomplish this with some examples:

Goal 1: Assess Evolving Cybersecurity Risks. For this, they list the main objective as follows: "Maintain strategic awareness of trends in national and systemic cybersecurity risks." The listed sub-objectives are to identify evolving cyber risks that affect national security, to identify and develop plans to address gaps in analytic and risk management capabilities in DHS, and lastly to develop scenarios and plans for future technology development and disruptive technologies. At the end of this, they list the outcomes from this goal: *"DHS understands national and systemic cybersecurity risks and regularly adjusts our program and policy efforts to account for evolving technologies and operational priorities."*[2] As a strategy goal, this is well-documented and has subitems to allow for folks who perform the execution some measurement on success. The objectives and sub-objectives are designed to help the constituents get to the desired outcome.

The challenge is in the execution of this strategy as the days, weeks, months, and years march by the cybersecurity and business teams. There are seven goals for the strategy. Which one, or more than one, does the organization pick as the "north star" to focus efforts on in the next few years? More specifically, the challenge is given to those who must execute their tactical and strategic goals when comparing it to these seven strategies (or goals).

---

[2] https://www.dhs.gov/sites/default/files/publications/DHS-Cybersecurity-Strategy_1.pdf p. 7

Next up is the Cybersecurity and Infrastructure Security Agency (CISA) Strategic Plan FY2024-2026.[3] It is improved in terms of its number of goals. The CISA lists three Cybersecurity Strategic Plan goals:

> ***GOAL 1: ADDRESS IMMEDIATE THREATS.*** *We will make it increasingly difficult for our adversaries to achieve their goals by targeting American and allied networks. We will work with partners to gain visibility into the breadth of intrusions targeting our country, enable the disruption of threat actor campaigns, ensure that adversaries are rapidly evicted when intrusions occur, and accelerate mitigation of exploitable conditions that adversaries recurringly exploit.*

> ***GOAL 2: HARDEN THE TERRAIN.*** *We will catalyze, support, and measure adoption of strong practices for security and resilience that measurably reduce the likelihood of damaging intrusions. We will provide actionable and usable guidance and direction that helps organizations prioritize the most effective security investments first and leverage scalable assessments to evaluate progress by organizations, critical infrastructure sectors, and the nation.*

> ***GOAL 3: DRIVE SECURITY AT SCALE.*** *We will drive prioritization of cybersecurity as a fundamental safety issue and ask more of technology providers to build security into products throughout their lifecycle, ship products with secure defaults, and foster radical transparency into their security practices so that customers clearly understand the risks they are accepting by using each product. Even as we confront the challenge of unsafe technology products, we must ensure that the future is more secure than the present—including by looking ahead to reduce the risks and fully leverage the benefits posed by artificial intelligence and the advance of quantum-relevant computing.*

---

[3] https://www.cisa.gov/sites/default/files/2023-08/FY2024-2026_ Cybersecurity_Strategic_Plan.pdf

Figure 3-1. *CISA Cybersecurity Strategic Plan Goals*

These are three good strategies or goals for CISA. What is more important and more inline with what the authors view as strategy is what they specifically state as their "north star":

OUR MISSION IS WELL-SUMMARIZED IN THE NATIONAL STRATEGY:

> *Defending the systems and assets that constitute our critical infrastructure is vital to our national security, public safety, and economic prosperity ... We aim to operationalize an enduring and effective model of collaborative defense that equitably distributes risk and responsibility and delivers a foundational level of security and resilience for our digital ecosystem.*

THIS IS OUR NORTH STAR.

The authors find this a much more compelling and useable strategy than the other three goals. One can argue whether it is the right strategy or not, and that is what most leadership organizations should be doing: having a healthy debate about what is their strategy, what is the measure of success for the strategy, and who owns its execution. The CISA authors mention one great caveat at the end of their north star statement that states "the environment may change, for tools and technology, and that may require us to reevaluate the strategy, but the statement of the strategy should be sufficient to make decisions."

Figure 3-2. *CISA Cybersecurity Strategic Plan Overview*

Looking at Figure 3-2, there are some objectives listed (like in the DHS example) of how to achieve each of the stated goals. They are short and, for the most part, measurable:

- Goal 1: Address Immediate Threats

- Objective 1.1: Increase visibility into, and ability to mitigate, cybersecurity threats and campaigns.

- Objective 1.2: Coordinate disclosure of, hunt for, and drive mitigation of critical and exploitable vulnerabilities.

- Objective 1.3: Plan for, exercise, and execute joint cyber defense operations and coordinate the response to significant cybersecurity incidents.

- Goal 2: Harden the Terrain

  - Objective 2.1: Understand how attacks really occur—and how to stop them.

  - Objective 2.2: Drive implementation of measurably effective cybersecurity investments.

  - Objective 2.3: Provide cybersecurity capabilities and services that fill gaps and help measure progress.

- Goal 3: Drive Security at Scale

  - Objective 3.1: Drive development of trustworthy technology products.

  - Objective 3.2: Understand and reduce the cybersecurity risks posed by emerging technologies.

  - Objective 3.3: Contribute to efforts to build a national cyber workforce.

And then, the document dives into how to measure the effectiveness of the strategic goals. On page 9 of the guide, there is a "Measure of Effectiveness" to enable the teams inside CISA to determine if they've accomplished this strategy. The measure of effectiveness of "Address Immediate Threats" is defined as

1. Reduction is the time to detect bad actor activity that affects federal agencies and critical infrastructure partners

2. Reduction in the time to remediation for every intrusion

3. Reduction in impact of incidents affecting CISA stakeholders

The reduction goals for measuring the effectiveness of the goal are designed to have a way to evaluate the amount of success. Provided the organization had existing statistics on current effectiveness of the same activities, they can evaluate their ability to meet their strategy.

There are some great wins in this strategy document. First, it has far fewer than the previous example from DHS, making it far easier to follow for adherence to the goals. More importantly, it formulates some measurements that enable the CISA team to understand how successful they are, not only at the end of the term but along the way so they can make adjustments as needed. The "north star" statement is additionally important as a way for all those engaged in CISA strategy to always look toward for success.

A third example is the State of Vermont Cybersecurity Strategy from 2019.[4] What is helpful in this strategy guide is that they leverage NIST Cybersecurity Framework (CSF) to align their strategy. We'll discuss this more in the example, but since many organizations also use NIST-CSF as their framework, this presents some easy examples for those in that space. Never reinvent the wheel.

---

[4]https://digitalservices.vermont.gov/sites/digitalservices/files/doc_library/Cybersecurity-Strategy.pdf

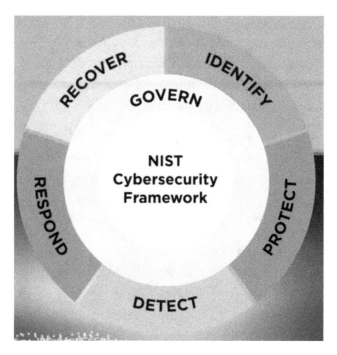

Figure 3-3. *NIST-CSF Wheel*

They list a series of "strategic principles":

- *Cyber Capability (NIST-CSF: Protect and Detect): Improve Vermont's digital security through increased knowledge, enhanced workforce development, and improved technology to protect and defend against, as well as reduce the risk of future cyberattacks.*

- *Cyber Resilience (NIST-CSF: Respond and Recover): Increase Vermont's ability to respond to and recover from cyber incidents. Decrease potential disruption, financial impact, intellectual property loss, and violation of privacy.*

- *Cyber Communication (NIST-CSF: Identify): Expand Vermont's communication, coordination, and awareness between entities such as state and local government agencies, businesses, and citizens to improve understanding of risk.*

- *Cyber Education (NIST-CSF: Protect): Build strong partnerships with local universities and colleges to enhance cyber education of Vermonters enabling the improvement of cyber capability, the expansion cyber communication, and the increased cyber resilience.*[5]

The document, much like the others, spends some time discussing the "problem statement": why it is necessary to have this strategy, and much of this is done with statistics on breaches and outages that have occurred. It is very effective as a way to instruct those who are not always familiar with how volatile this area can be, bringing them into "the know."

The document provides a scope statement, which is very helpful and one we'd encourage as a way to set the parameters for how far this scope is applicable. It also lists the potential and required collaborators for the success of the strategy. To achieve the strategic principles listed above, the document then outlines the items they will accomplish to ensure success. Rather than listing all of those in this book, feel free to review and see how they match the strategic principles listed above.

The state of Vermont has a similar approach to the CISA document "north star" in that it lists a mission and vision:

- State of Vermont Cyber Mission: To improve Vermont's cybersecurity

---

[5] https://digitalservices.vermont.gov/sites/digitalservices/files/doc_library/Cybersecurity-Strategy.pdf p. 3–4

- State Vermont Cyber Vision: A cyber secure and resilient Vermont where it is safe to live, work, and play

As stated, very similar to the "north star" statement from CISA and can serve the same purpose: a very succinct statement of what will guide all decisions going forward. There will be specifics to do in order to accomplish the mission and vision; however, those two statements are also great synonyms for Strategy.

Strategy Build 101

We've explored some examples of how other organizations have tackled and published their own cybersecurity strategy. These examples are listed as a way to take what has been a largely theoretical discussion into how actual teams are developing strategy. Of course, many larger organizations will look to management consultants to come in and help them develop a strategy. Often, this involves senior cyber leadership and relevant business leaders getting into an offsite so they can focus on this heads-down work. For those teams who cannot afford this type of engagement or are able to do this "in-house," we will provide some easy steps for strategy building in case none of the examples ring close enough to your situation.

A quick refresh, why is a strategy important? Because many organizations, especially cybersecurity- and technology-related groups, find themselves often in very reactive mode, developing a strategy (with a focus on areas of risk and concern) steers an organization from a state of constant firefighting into one where the reactions are far less surprising and scary.

Step 1: Assessment

In this first step, the organization is assessing two items. First is to understand the scope and risk of your cyber threat landscape. This varies, naturally, by industry, size, geo-location, and hundreds of other factors. Examine what types of threats your organization faces currently and potentially in the next few years. As the team is making this list of threats, it should always have in mind a risk-based approach. In fact, the whole team developing the strategy must have a risk-based approach. This means not all risk is created equally, and so as risks, threats, vulnerabilities, and others are identified, there should be an effort to list them in risk-order to the enterprise. Ensure your threat intelligence team is informing this early team on upcoming threats so the strategy has legs and doesn't get stale too quickly.

The next assessment is your own program's cybersecurity maturity. What framework is the organization aligned to (NIST-CSF, ISO 27001, CSA, etc.) that it can use to measure the performance. Ensure the review encompasses all the organizational elements such as governance, risk, and compliance (GRC), policies, security technologies, incident response, and disaster recovery capabilities. At the end of this review, when a maturity level is determined, the leadership would select a goal maturity level within a given time frame (2–5 years). A word of note: five years can be a long time in technology and cybersecurity, so the authors would recommend as short as period as the team is comfortable. As you evaluate your current cybersecurity maturity, the team will identify "gaps" as in risk reduction programs, process, technologies, or resources that are identified as the improvements needed.

Let's take an example to help illustrate how it would work. As part of the initial assessment for the threat landscape, the organization identifies that ransomware will be the largest threat to the team in the next three years. This organization is NIST-CSF framework-aligned. The parts of NIST-CSF that best match the risk from ransomware are found in a couple of areas in the framework:

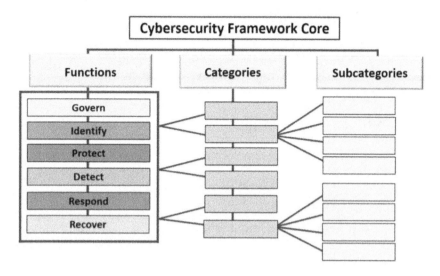

Figure 3-4. *NIST-CSF Framework Graphic*

- NIST-CSF: Protect (PR)

  - NIST-CSF.PR.AT: Awareness and Training

    - PR.AT-1: All users are informed and trained.

    - PR.AT-2: Privileged users understand their roles and responsibilities.

    - PR.AT-3: Third-party stakeholders (e.g., suppliers, customers, partners) understand their roles and responsibilities.

    - PR.AT-4: Senior executives understand their roles and responsibilities.

    - PR.AT-5: Physical and cybersecurity personnel understand their roles and responsibilities.

- NIST-CSF.PR.DS: Data Security

  - RP.DS-6: Integrity-checking mechanisms are used to verify software, firmware, and information integrity.

- NIST-CSF: Detect (DE)

  - NIST-CSF.DE.AE: Anomalies and Events

    - DE.AE-1: A baseline of network operations and expected data flows for users and systems is established and managed.

    - DE.AE-2: Detected events are analyzed to understand attack targets and methods.

    - DE.AE-3: Event data are collected and correlated from multiple sources and sensors.

    - DE.AE-4: Impact of events is determined.

    - DE.AE-5: Incident alert thresholds are established.

  - NIST-CSF.DE.CM: Security Continuous Monitoring

    - DE.AE-1: A baseline of network operations and expected data flows for users and systems is established and managed.

    - DE.AE-2: Detected events are analyzed to understand attack targets and methods.

    - DE.AE-3: Event data are collected and correlated from multiple sources and sensors.

    - DE.AE-4: Impact of events is determined.

    - DE.AE-5: Incident alert thresholds are established.

- NIST-CSF.DE.DP: Detection Processes

  - DE.65: Incident alert thresholds are established.

- NIST-CSF: Respond (RE)

  - NIST-CSF.RS.RP: Response Planning

    - RS.RP-1: Response plan is executed during or after an incident.

- NIST-CSF.RS.CO: Communications

  - RS.CO-1: Personnel know their roles and order of operations when a response is needed.

  - RS.CO-2: Incidents are reported consistent with established criteria.

  - RS.CO-3: Information is shared consistent with response plans.

  - RS.CO-4: Coordination with stakeholders occurs consistent with response plans.

  - RS.CO-5: Voluntary information sharing occurs with external stakeholders to achieve broader cybersecurity situational awareness.

- NIST-CSF.RS.AN: Analysis

  - RS.AN-1: Notifications from detection systems are investigated.

  - RS.AN-2: The impact of the incident is understood.

  - RS.AN-3: Forensics are performed.

  - RS.AN-4: Incidents are categorized consistent with response plans.

- RS.AN-5: Processes are established to receive, analyze, and respond to vulnerabilities disclosed to the organization from internal and external sources (e.g., internal testing, security bulletins, or security researchers).

- NIST-CSF.RS.MI: Mitigation

  - RS.MI-1: Incidents are contained.

  - RS.MI-2: Incidents are mitigated.

  - RS.MI-3: Newly identified vulnerabilities are mitigated or documented as accepted risks.

- NIST-CSF.RS.IM: Improvements

  - RS.IM-1: Response plans incorporate lessons learned.

  - RS.IM-2: Response strategies are updated.

These are the relevant controls and descriptions in NIST-CSF that correspond to the threat from ransomware. You could include some of the identity and recover too, but we are going to draw the line at the above list for the sake of brevity and to make the point that the organization can't make everything a priority. Focus on the areas that need the most improvement, and in this example, the organization determines that identity and recover are mature "enough." They may do work on them to improve them, but they will be lower on the risk decision-making ladder.

Step 2: Risk-Based Improvements

The completion of "Step 1: Assessment" will produce a list of risks, threats, and issues from the gaps in where the organization currently is in the framework and where it needs to be to meet the goal. The lists are usually quite long and can be a challenge just to collate. However, the requirement for any organization or team is to always take the risk-based approach in how the list is documented and executed.

Authors' Note: We are going to contradict ourselves a bit here on a risk-based approach. A risk-based list still needs to be developed and published. However, based upon our experience, there are two situations where you could go out of order:

- Easy Win: As the list is reviewed, there may be some issues or risks that require very little work to accomplish a significant improvement in the maturity score. Make a note of these instances, if any exist, as the list is managed, and be ready to discuss if it makes sense to do those out of order.

- Major Gap: this is a rare outlier case, but when this occurs, there is a risk that has a high probability of being exploited, but it did not make it high on your list in risk-based order. This isn't a zero-day vulnerability issue or exploit as this describes a situation during planning: as the list is being created, the team identifies some software vulnerability related to the risk that has a high CVSS score (for example), but that risk is not high on the risk-based list in relation to the risk of the software vulnerability.

These are the two examples in "the wild" the authors have witnessed in doing the risk-based approach that involves looking for the above examples that might need to go out of order. They are not common, and don't expect a lot of them, but keep an eye out for targets of opportunity.

To continue with the example, the team looks at the several NIST-CSF categories and subcategories to develop the list of gaps and risks. Then, the team needs to be sure to include not just cybersecurity but include the business (who does cybersecurity "service"?) and other relevant leaders who can understand and opine toward the risk-based approach. It shouldn't be isolated to cyber but must include others to ensure all risks are considered, not just cyber risk. Why not just cyber risk? Because any cyber incident, in particular a ransomware attack, will require the involvement of other risk domains: legal, corporate communications, privacy, and others.

As this team works through the list of gaps identified, it will make a list in risk-based order. This assessment should follow an existing process at your organization for how cyber and other risks are identified and measured. This list must be placed in a "system of record" (this is defined as the data management system used as the authoritative source for risk data at your organization) for tracking. As the organization provides a risk rating and places them in order inside the system of record, this list becomes the targets to complete in order to accomplish the strategy. In most organizations, these can be labeled as "findings" or "gaps" that need attention to successfully reach the goals of the strategy.

Step 3: Document Strategy

Documenting strategy is the act of taking the risk-based list, now placed in the organization's risk management system of record, and disseminating that out to the rest of the organization as the goals for the set period of time. Assigning owners to each of the findings/gaps with clear remediation plans that have firm dates is required. Ensure each of these not only has an owner but that the owners are responsible for the successful completion of them. If the risk/gap/finding is of high enough risk to the team, it must also require an "urgent risk mitigation" plan. This "urgent risk mitigation" plan is designed to lower the risk with whatever means available (detective, reactive, or other) to lower the risk until the full remediation plan can be implemented.

Step 4: Reassessment

The last step is to recognize that a strategy, like any other long-term project or program, needs to be periodically re-evaluated for appropriateness and effectiveness. As the team makes progress on each of the findings/ risks and then presumably makes progress on the strategy, there needs to be checkpoints whether the team is on target. Taking the individual goals to accomplish (the findings to be closed in the risk system of record) along with gauging if it had the expected impact on the strategy goals is the outcome from the reassessment step. How often this re-evaluation happens depends on the teams decisions, but at a minimum, it should be once a year. The authors' recommendation would be at least twice a year, to allow for changing of priorities and risks as needed without too much "churn" or staring at the issue too long.

These four steps are the basic steps to creating a strategy at any organization. Important items to keep in mind are the need to make the strategy decisions within a larger team as appropriate, ensure the strategy arrived upon is simple enough to be understood by those performing the work, and lastly be ready to review the work as it progresses to make adjustments.

4-Step Strategy Guide

Figure 3-5. *Cybersecurity Strategy Wheel*

The Importance of Frameworks and Standards

There has been a number of discussions and parts of this, and other books, that deal with frameworks. While many readers are familiar with them, there can be the question of why the reliance on frameworks so much? What makes them so important and why do the authors keep referencing them so much.

What is the purpose of a framework? A framework is designed to provide an infrastructure (predefined structure), rules, and guides for those implementing to build a system, control, or process. The framework allows an engineer, developer, designer, and other roles to build upon these predefined structures and thus reduce the need to build from scratch. The old saying "why reinvent the wheel" is part of the rationale for the framework.

A framework also ensures organizations do not forget important parts of a control or system to control. For example, when a corporation settles on NIST-CSF as their cybersecurity framework, the cybersecurity team will leverage the NIST-CSF framework when creating their policy and standards. As the teams create these policies and standards, there will be checks against the NIST-CSF framework to ensure they've covered all appropriate controls in their enterprise. Without a framework to design their cybersecurity program and to develop policies and standards internally, then the program and policies are likely to be a list of best practices, without a "predefined structure" that is characteristic of a framework approach. One thing that is guaranteed in an approach without a framework: at least one, if not more, control will be missed, and thus, the whole program is at risk due to that miss (or misses).

Lastly, the use of a framework ensures that the organization can reuse existing resources. A framework, in the role of a predefined structure, will an organization that leverages it being able to recognize resources that can be reused across the enterprise. Without a framework, these resources can look very dissimilar and disconnected; however, a framework such as NIST-CSF or ISO 27001 will point out to practitioners the connectivity of controls and resources to leverage.

The end result of these three outcomes from adopting a framework: improved productivity and lower risk. The predefined structure allows easier reuse of resources and easier collaboration across pillars internally. The structure created by a framework can seem overly simplistic, and at times, the controls can have a sort of "duh" to them as they are obvious to cyber professionals as needed items. However, not everyone is a cyber expert, and tying your program and controls back to a framework gives the enterprise the assurance there is both a rhyme and reason for the way the program and controls are structured.

Current State

Discovery Process and/or Tool

Joiners, Movers, and Leavers

Cleanup

NIST-CSF 2.0

The National Institute of Standards and Technology Cybersecurity Framework (NIST-CSF) was originally published in 2014 and set a guideline for how organizations can lower the information technology and cybersecurity risks in the enterprise. Ten years later, in 2024, NIST released the updated version (2.0) for a major update to the framework. The update was sorely needed as the time from COVID-19 and forward have seen a huge increase in cyber risk.

The authors are aware there are other frameworks but have selected NIST-CSF as the example in the book because there is ample mapping from it to other frameworks. For those mappings, go to the CSF 2.0 Informative References page on the NIST website.[6] If you're organization uses ISO 27001 or other frameworks, use this page and accompanying spreadsheets to work from NIST-CSF to the matching in the framework of your choice.

The other reason for the choice of NIST-CSF 2.0 is the utility provided: CSF 2.0 Reference Tool.[7] The tool allows organizations to develop strategy in conjunction with the framework with a customizable access to the framework's core components. The original purpose of NIST-CSF was the protection of critical infrastructure, but NIST has expanded it to include nearly all organizations (the NIST Small Business guidance is geared to that small business sector, and we will deal it in the next section).

Very importantly to the framework is an additional function "Govern" that was added as a sixth core function. The others were already there: Identify, Protect, Detect, Respond, and Recover. As the team looks at the updated NIST-CSF 2.0 graphic below, what is striking is this new function of "Govern" sits underneath all the other five functions. This calls out that governance aims to improve the operation of risk management and decision-making in the enterprise. Calling out the Govern function as underlying the whole wheel of functions is a much-needed callout and a very welcome addition.

---

[6]https://www.nist.gov/informative-references
[7]https://www.nist.gov/cyberframework

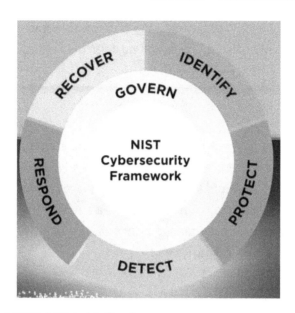

Figure 3-6. *NIST-CSF 2.0 Wheel*

Focusing on what is relevant in this framework for Identity and Access Management and Privileged Access Management programs is the next step. Because IAM systems are the underlying controls for a PAM program, the updates in this section are important. There was a large update to the Identify function to expand its scope and controls. It focuses on effectively managing digital identities which are crucial to lowering risk. Expanding the Identify section of the framework, it strives to assist with the expansion of digital identities and access, many areas where privilege is required, and the blurring of the lines between privileged and non-privileged accounts.

As the organization leverages NIST-CSF to assess their current PAM maturity and then perform gap analysis, the following sections are most important to the PAM and IAM areas. Read it as the Functions are at the top level, with the Categories next and Subcategories listed as the last bullets. If the Category and/or the Subcategory is missing in the list below, then it is the opinion of the authors it is not directly relevant to an assessment of a PAM program. If the Category is listed, the relevant Subcategories will be listed. There will be a further explanation of relevance and context where needed.

Identify (ID)

Identify function in the wheel requires the organization to understand the current risks to the enterprise. This includes all the business context, resources required to support, and their related cyber risks. The understanding is required to ensure there is an ability to prioritize efforts and that it matches the risk management strategy. In the PAM systems, there should be the following focus.

Asset Management (ID.AM)

- *"Assets (e.g., data, hardware, software, systems, facilities, services, people) that enable the organization to achieve business purposes are identified and managed consistent with their relative importance to organizational objectives and the organization's risk strategy."* PAM, as part of the larger process involving people, process, and technology, will assist in the identification and management of the accounts and systems that have elevated access; in addition, it will ensure these accounts are cataloged and monitored.

  - ID.AM-02: *Inventories of software, services, and systems managed by the organization are maintained.*

  - ID.AM-03: *Representations of the organization's authorized network communication and internal and external network data flows are maintained.*

- ID.AM-04: *Inventories of services provided by suppliers are maintained.*

- ID.AM-05: *Assets are prioritized based on classification, criticality, resources, and impact on the mission.*

Risk Assessment (ID.RA)

- *The cybersecurity risk to the organization, assets, and individuals is understood by the organization.* In this control, the Privileged Access Management, along with other people, process, and technology, will assist in identifying risks with elevated accounts, from both insiders and those external threats to the enterprise. An example of people, process, and technology in the domain is an active asset management policy and program.

Improvement (ID.IM)

- *Improvements to organizational cybersecurity risk management processes, procedures, and activities are identified across all CSF functions.*

  - ID.IM-01: *Improvements are identified from evaluations.*

  - ID.IM-02: *Improvements are identified from security tests and exercises, including those done in coordination with suppliers and relevant third parties.*

  - ID.IM-03: *Improvements are identified from execution of operational processes, procedures, and activities.*

Protect (PR)

The Protect function is designed to focus the enterprise on the safeguards to defend or prevent attacks. Protect category covers access controls, user awareness and training, data security, and information protections. It also includes a section on maintenance to ensure the Protect function is continuous. *"Safeguards to manage the organization's cybersecurity risks are used."*

Access Control (PR.AA)

Identity Management, Authentication, and Access Control (PR.AA): Access to physical and logical assets is limited to authorized users, services, and hardware and managed commensurate with the assessed risk of unauthorized access.

- *PR.AA-01: Identities and credentials for authorized users, services, and hardware are managed by the organization.*

- *PR.AA-02: Identities are proofed and bound to credentials based on the context of interactions.*

- *PR.AA-03: Users, services, and hardware are authenticated.*

- *PR.AA-04: Identity assertions are protected, conveyed, and verified.*

- *PR.AA-05: Access permissions, entitlements, and authorizations are defined in a policy, managed, enforced, and reviewed and incorporate the principles of least privilege and separation of duties.*

- *PR.AA-06: Physical access to assets is managed, monitored, and enforced commensurate with risk.*

Privileged Access Management systems are a crucial part of the overall solution (other IAM solutions, physical access systems, etc.) for controlling access to elevated accounts, ensuring only the appropriate and authorized gain access, and at the time and duration required.

Awareness and Training (PR.AT)

Awareness and Training (PR.AT): The organization's personnel are provided with cybersecurity awareness and training so that they can perform their cybersecurity-related tasks.

- *PR.AT-01: Personnel are provided with awareness and training so that they possess the knowledge and skills to perform general tasks with cybersecurity risks in mind.*

- *PR.AT-02: Individuals in specialized roles are provided with awareness and training so that they possess the knowledge and skills to perform relevant tasks with cybersecurity risks in mind.*

There is a need to ensure the policies and requirements for privileged accounts are well communicated and learned in the organization. There should be a robust training and awareness program that includes PAM as appropriate for job roles and functions.

Platform Security (PR.DS)

Platform Security (PR.DS): The hardware, software (e.g., firmware, operating systems, applications), and services of physical and virtual platforms are managed consistent with the organization's risk strategy to protect their confidentiality, integrity, and availability.

- *PR.DS-01: Configuration management practices are established and applied.*

- *Ex2: Review all default configuration settings that may potentially impact cybersecurity when installing or upgrading software.*

- *PR.DS-04: Log records are generated and made available for continuous monitoring.*

  - *Ex1: Configure all operating systems, applications, and services (including cloud-based services) to generate log records.*

  - *Ex2: Configure log generators to securely share their logs with the organization's logging infrastructure systems and services.*

  - *Ex3: Configure log generators to record the data needed by Zero Trust architectures.*

- *PR.PS-05: Installation and execution of unauthorized software are prevented.*

  - *Ex1: When risk warrants it, restrict software execution to permitted products only, or deny the execution of prohibited and unauthorized software.*

  - *Ex2: Verify the source of new software and the software's integrity before installing it.*

  - *Ex3: Configure platforms to use only approved DNS services that block access to known malicious domains.*

  - *Ex4: Configure platforms to allow the installation of organization-approved software only.*

- *PR.PS-06: Secure software development practices are integrated, and their performance is monitored throughout the software development life cycle.*

  - *Ex1: Protect all components of organization-developed software from tampering and unauthorized access.*

The security of platforms in the enterprise is reliant on the success of PAM. By ensuring the access and control of these platform is appropriate with the users/systems permissions, this guarantees the platforms are secure.

Technology Infrastructure Resilience (PR.IR)

Technology Infrastructure Resilience (PR.IR): Security architectures are managed with the organization's risk strategy to protect asset confidentiality, integrity, and availability and organizational resilience.

- *PR.IR-01: Networks and environments are protected from unauthorized logical access and usage.*

  - *Ex2: Logically segment organization networks from external networks, and permit only necessary communications to enter the organization's networks from the external networks.*

The resilience of technology infrastructure, much like the Data and Platform Security subcategories, is dependent upon PAM implementation. Privileged Access Management (PAM) enhances organizational resilience by reducing the Attack Surface, mitigating risks associated with privileged accounts, and improving incident response capabilities. PAM achieves this by controlling and monitoring access to sensitive systems and data, ensuring that only authorized users have the necessary privileges, and providing comprehensive auditing and logging. The prevention of unauthorized logical access is central to PAM's success.

Overall, the Protect function in NIST-CSF when evaluated against PAM focuses on access controls, awareness and training, and the security of platforms, data, and infrastructure.

Detect (DE)

DETECT (DE): Possible cybersecurity attacks and compromises are found and analyzed. In this function, the goal is to have systems that identify when the occurrence of negative cyber events.

Continuous Monitoring (DE.CM)

Continuous Monitoring (DE.CM): Assets are monitored to find anomalies, indicators of compromise, and other potentially adverse events.

- *DE.CM-01: Networks and network services are monitored to find potentially adverse events.*

    - *Ex4: Compare actual network flows against baselines to detect deviations.*

    - *Ex5: Monitor network communications to identify changes in security postures for Zero Trust purposes.*

- *DE.CM-03: Personnel activity and technology usage are monitored to find potentially adverse events.*

    - *Ex1: Use behavior analytics software to detect anomalous user activity to mitigate insider threats.*

    - *Ex2: Monitor logs from logical access control systems to find unusual access patterns and failed access attempts.*

    - *Ex3: Continuously monitor deception technology, including user accounts, for any usage.*

- *DE.CM-06: External service provider activities and services are monitored to find potentially adverse events.*

  - *Ex1: Monitor remote and on-site administration and maintenance activities that external providers perform on organizational systems.*

  - *Ex2: Monitor activity from cloud-based services, Internet service providers, and other service providers for deviations from expected behavior.*

- *DE.CM-09: Computing hardware and software, runtime environments, and their data are monitored to find potentially adverse events.*

  - *Ex2: Monitor authentication attempts to identify attacks against credentials and unauthorized credential reuse.*

  - *Ex5: Use technologies with a presence on endpoints to detect cyber health issues (e.g., missing patches, malware infections, unauthorized software), and redirect the endpoints to a remediation environment before access is authorized.*

Privileged Access Management systems must provide for continuous monitoring of elevated account activity and provide for real-time alerts when suspicious activities occur. Privileged Access Management (PAM) enables continuous monitoring of privileged users by logging and analyzing their activities in real time, detecting anomalies, and triggering alerts. This constant vigilance helps identify suspicious or unauthorized actions, enhancing the organization's ability to respond to potential security threats, including insider threats.

115

Adverse Event Analysis (DE.AE)

Adverse Event Analysis (DE.AE): Anomalies, indicators of compromise, and other potentially adverse events are analyzed to characterize the events and detect cybersecurity incidents.

- *DE.AE-06: Information on adverse events is provided to authorized staff and tools.*

    - *Ex1: Use cybersecurity software to generate alerts and provide them to the security operations center (SOC), incident responders, and incident response tools.*

    - *Ex2: Incident responders and other authorized personnel can access log analysis findings at all times.*

    - *Ex3: Automatically create and assign tickets in the organization's ticketing system when certain types of alerts occur.*

    - *Ex4: Manually create and assign tickets in the organization's ticketing system when technical staff discover indicators of compromise.*

In order for PAM to be successful, there must be a process to detect anomalous behavior on privileged accounts through other complementary processes in information technology and cybersecurity. Because of the value of privileged accounts to attackers, getting these identified and escalated is crucial.

Respond (RS)

RESPOND (RS): Actions regarding a detected cybersecurity incident are taken. The function of Respond is to ensure all the activities to detect cybersecurity events, incidents, and breaches. The overview covers incident management, analysis, and then mitigation.

Incident Management (RS.MA)

Incident Management (RS.MA): Responses to detected cybersecurity incidents are managed.

- *RS.MA-03: Incidents are categorized and prioritized.*

Incident management is assisted by PAM by relaying access information on the systems affected.

Incident Analysis (RS.AN)

Incident Analysis (RS.AN): Investigations are conducted to ensure effective response and support forensics and recovery activities.

- *RS.AN-03: Analysis is performed to establish what has taken place during an incident and the root cause of the incident.*

When PAM is correctly implemented and managed, then the analysis of incidents that involved an elevated account are optimized. It also ensures the correct level of logging and monitoring is taking place to be able to analyze the appropriate data.

Incident Mitigation (RS.MI)

Incident Mitigation (RS.MI): Activities are performed to prevent the expansion of an event and mitigate its effects.

- *RS.MI-01: Incidents are contained.*

  - *Ex1: Cybersecurity technologies (e.g., antivirus software) and cybersecurity features of other technologies (e.g., operating systems, network infrastructure devices) automatically perform containment action.*

When an event or breach occurs, Privileged Access Management is critical to revoking access or shutting down compromised systems to limit the damage and lateral movement of the bad actors.

Recover (RC)

Recover (RC): Assets and operations affected by a cybersecurity incident are restored. The function of Recover is to identify the actions and plans for resilience and restoration of services after an incident.

Incident Recovery Plan Execution (RC.RP)

Incident Recovery Plan Execution (RC.RP): Restoration activities are performed to ensure operational availability of systems and services affected by cybersecurity incidents. The function of Recover is to identify the actions and activities required to maintain plans for resilience and restoration of capabilities after an incident.

- *RC.RP-01: The recovery portion of the incident response plan is executed once initiated from the incident response process.*

  - *Ex1: Begin recovery procedures during or after incident response processes.*

  - *Ex2: Make all individuals with recovery responsibilities aware of the plans for recovery and the authorizations required to implement each aspect of the plans.*

- *RC.RP-03: The integrity of backups and other restoration assets is verified before using them for restoration.*

- *RC.RP-04: Critical mission functions and cybersecurity risk management are considered to establish post-incident operational norms.*

Privileged Access Management is an important part of recovery planning by safeguarding access to sensitive or critical systems can be restored after an incident. Privileged Access Management (PAM) significantly enhances recovery planning by providing better control, visibility, and auditability, especially in the event of a security incident. PAM helps organizations identify and address the root cause of an incident more quickly and efficiently, limiting the potential for further damage and speeding up the recovery process.

Govern (GV)

Govern (GV): The organization's cybersecurity risk management strategy, expectations, and policy are established, communicated, and monitored. The Govern function is listed last in our list because the authors view it as the most important and because it "covers" the rest of the five functions. Govern encompasses the how a program is planned and operated in a controlled and secure manner.

Organizational Context (GV.OC)

Organizational Context (GV.OC): The circumstances—mission, stakeholder expectations, dependencies, and legal, regulatory, and contractual requirements—surrounding the organization's cybersecurity risk management decisions are understood. Organization context is important for PAM to be able to understand who, what, where, and how risks are identified and prioritized and how PAM can address those risks.

- *GV.OC-01: The organizational mission is understood and informs cybersecurity risk management.*

  - *Ex1: Share the organization's mission (e.g., through vision and mission statements, marketing, and service strategies) to provide a basis for identifying risks that may impede that mission.*

- *GV.OC-04: Critical objectives, capabilities, and services that external stakeholders depend on or expect from the organization are understood and communicated.*

- *GV.OC-05: Outcomes, capabilities, and services that the organization depends on are understood and communicated.*

PAM is an important part of organizational context to assist in the correct risk rating of subjects and resources.

Risk Management Strategy (GV.RM)

Risk Management Strategy (GV.RM): The organization's priorities, constraints, risk tolerance and appetite statements, and assumptions are established, communicated, and used to support operational risk decisions.

- *GV.RM-02: Risk appetite and risk tolerance statements are established, communicated, and maintained.*

- *GV.RM-03: Cybersecurity risk management activities and outcomes are included in enterprise risk management processes.*

Privileged Access Management is part of the risk management strategy because elevated accounts and their management are high-risk items. Privileged Access Management (PAM) significantly enhances risk management strategies by reducing the Attack Surface, improving threat detection, and minimizing the impact of potential breaches. PAM focuses on securing and controlling access to sensitive resources, ensuring only authorized individuals have the necessary privileges at the right time, and implementing mechanisms to monitor and audit their activities.

Roles, Responsibilities, and Authorities (GV.RR)

Roles, Responsibilities, and Authorities (GV.RR): Cybersecurity roles, responsibilities, and authorities to foster accountability, performance assessment, and continuous improvement are established and communicated.

- *GV.RR-02: Roles, responsibilities, and authorities related to cybersecurity risk management are established, communicated, understood, and enforced.*

  - *Ex5: Clearly articulate cybersecurity responsibilities within operations, risk functions, and internal audit functions.*

- *GV.RR-04: Cybersecurity is included in human resources practices.*

  - *Ex1: Integrate cybersecurity risk management considerations into human resources processes (e.g., personnel screening, onboarding, change notification, offboarding).*

  - *Ex2: Consider cybersecurity knowledge to be a positive factor in hiring, training, and retention decisions.*

- *Ex3: Conduct background checks prior to onboarding new personnel for sensitive roles, and periodically repeat background checks for personnel with such roles.*

- *Ex4: Define and enforce obligations for personnel to be aware of, adhere to, and uphold security policies as they relate to their roles.*

Within the Govern function, the roles and responsibilities are the most aligned to PAM strategy and tactics. Ensure the polices, roles, and other factors in this section align with PAM and the outcomes.

Policy (GV.PO)

Policy (GV.PO): Organizational cybersecurity policy is established, communicated, and enforced.

- *GV.PO-01: Policy for managing cybersecurity risks is established based on organizational context, cybersecurity strategy, and priorities and is communicated and enforced.*

- *GV.PO-02: Policy for managing cybersecurity risks is reviewed, updated, communicated, and enforced to reflect changes in requirements, threats, technology, and organizational mission.*

Policy is a crucial part of any PAM deployment and success. This area needs good attention that the policies are published and clearly written. A strong Privileged Access Management (PAM) policy is crucial for organizational success because it safeguards critical systems, reduces Attack Surfaces, and enables organizations to comply with regulatory requirements. By controlling and managing access to sensitive resources, PAM minimizes the risk of data breaches and operational disruptions while also streamlining security operations and improving overall efficiency.

Oversight (GV.OV)

Oversight (GV.OV): Results of organization-wide cybersecurity risk management activities and performance are used to inform, improve, and adjust the risk management strategy.

Oversight of PAM is important to the success to ensure nothing is missed and improvements can be made as needed.

Cybersecurity Supply Chain Risk Management (GV.SC)

Cybersecurity Supply Chain Risk Management (GV.SC): Cyber supply chain risk management processes are identified, established, managed, monitored, and improved by organizational stakeholders.

- *GV.SC-02: Cybersecurity roles and responsibilities for suppliers, customers, and partners are established, communicated, and coordinated internally and externally.*

- *GV.SC-05: Requirements to address cybersecurity risks in supply chains are established, prioritized, and integrated into contracts and other types of agreements with suppliers and other relevant third parties.*

- *GV.SC-06: Planning and due diligence are performed to reduce risks before entering into formal supplier or other third-party relationships.*

- *GV.SC-07: The risks posed by a supplier, their products and services, and other third parties are understood, recorded, prioritized, assessed, responded to, and monitored over the course of the relationship.*

- *GV.SC-09: Supply chain security practices are integrated into cybersecurity and enterprise risk management programs, and their performance is monitored throughout the technology product and service life cycle.*

Suppliers, also known as third parties or vendors, are often high risk due to the nature of the data they process or connections to the organization's enterprise. Privileged Access Management must be part of any supplier and/or third-party risk program to lower the risk they present. A robust Privileged Access Management (PAM) policy is crucial for mitigating third-party risk because it provides visibility, control, and auditability over privileged access, especially for vendors who might have access to sensitive systems and data. This helps prevent unauthorized access, reduces the risk of insider threats, and ensures compliance with regulations.

NIST Small Business Guidance

NIST-CSF and other similar framework, such as ISO 27000 series or NIST 800-53, are excellent frameworks and extensively used globally. However, they are a challenge for small businesses. In fact, one could reasonably argue that those frameworks are overkill and will drown the small business owner or team into work that does not produce value.

NISTIR 7621 Revision 1, Small Business Information Security: The Fundamentals

Luckily for the authors and for small business owners, NIST has developed a framework for this sector: NISTIR 7621 Revision 1, Small Business Information Security: The Fundamentals.[8] It is aligned to NIST-CSF version 1, not 2, so the Governance function is missing. This is due to it being published in 2017, but we do cover the updated version in NIST-CSF 2.0 in case the organization is able to align to the updated version.

The publication has some excellent guides for small business owners on how to calculate:

---

[8] https://nvlpubs.nist.gov/nistpubs/ir/2016/nist.ir.7621r1.pdf

- Risk

- Determine critical information and users

- Worksheet to determine impact if an incident or breach

- Asset inventory examples

- Basic threat modeling

- Covers the NIST-CSF 1.0 framework in basic
  business terms

There are categories and tasks called out in the guidance by the NIST-CSF functions that are relevant to PAM:

- Identify:

  - Identify and control who has access to your
    business information.

  - Require individual user accounts for each
    employee.

  - Create policies and procedures for information
    security.

- Protect:

  - Limit employee access to data and information.

  - Install and activate software and hardware firewalls
    on all your business networks.

  - Secure your wireless access points and networks.

  - Set up web and email filters.

  - Use encryption for sensitive data.

  - Train your employees.

- Detect:

    - Install and update antivirus, antispyware, and other anti-malware programs.

    - Maintain and monitor logs.

- Respond:

    - Develop a plan for disasters and information security incidents.

- Recover:

    - Make full backups of important business information.

    - Make improvement to processes/procedures/ technologies.

Outside of the framework for small business, it provides some other great nuggets that are related to elevated account security.

- Use strong passwords: It recommends using a random sequence of letters, numbers, and special characters that are at least 12 characters long.

- Change default passwords: It recommends looking for default administration accounts with passwords.

- Passwords should be changed at least every three months.

    - A note from the authors (and technical reviewer): While this is the recommendation of NIST for small businesses, we strongly disagree with the rotation of passwords because it encourages poor password selection. Rather, it would be better to use a password generator and vaulting tool that drastically lowers the risk of password compromise. There are a tons of free and paid solutions in this space that are bound to meet the price and criteria for any small business.

- Passwords should not be shared.

This publication is a bit dated and is starting to show its age when compared to the updated NIST-CSF 2.0 small business recommendations. However, there are some basics that haven't changed, and the authors would still recommend it. If the small business is looking for an update framework that has some great resources, then NIST has done some work to make CSF 2.0 approachable to this business size.

NIST-CSF 2.0 for Small Business

NIST has updated the guidance for small businesses in their updated release of NIST-CSF. The authors list the NISTIR 7621 because it is a bit more comprehensive and specific in some areas that this advice misses or doesn't do as good a job. However, we will cover how a small business owner can leverage this framework effectively.

One of the best updates is NIST has added a specific webpage "Small Business Security Corner[9]" where there are a lot of resources and guides. Highly recommended to bookmark this page if you fit in this business size category. On this page are links to the framework guidance for small business, some quick-start guides, and also videos. If you run a small business, this landing page is a great place to start.

---

[9] https://www.nist.gov/itl/smallbusinesscyber

The NIST-CSF 2.0 Small Business Quick-Start Guide[10] (is also called NIST SP 1300) was published in February 2024. This guidance provides for the Govern function along with the other five functions. Like the older version above, it lists the functions with several specific items that are relevant to PAM:

- Govern:
    - Understand how cybersecurity risks can disrupt the achievement of your business's mission.
    - Understand who within your business will be responsible for developing and executing the cybersecurity strategy.
    - Assess the potential impact of a total or partial loss of critical business assets and operations.
    - Assess cybersecurity risks posed by suppliers and other third parties before entering into formal relationships.
    - Communicate, enforce, and maintain policies for managing cybersecurity risks.

- Identify:
    - Understand what assets your business relies upon by creating and maintaining an inventory of hardware, software, systems, and services.
    - Assess your assets (IT and physical) for potential vulnerabilities.

---

[10] https://nvlpubs.nist.gov/nistpubs/SpecialPublications/NIST.SP.1300.pdf

- Assess the effectiveness of the business's cybersecurity program to identify areas that need improvement.

- Prioritize inventorying and classifying your business data.

- Prioritize documenting internal and external cybersecurity threats and associated responses using a risk register.

- Communicate cybersecurity plans, policies, and best practices to all staff and relevant third parties.

- Protect:

  - Understand what information employees should or do have access to. Restrict sensitive information access to only those employees who need it to do their jobs.

  - Assess the timeliness, quality, and frequency of your company's cybersecurity training for employees.

  - Prioritize requiring multifactor authentication on all accounts that offer it.

  - Consider using password managers to help you and your staff generate and protect strong passwords.

  - Prioritize changing default manufacturer passwords.

  - Prioritize regularly updating and patching software and operating systems. Enable automatic updates to help you remember.

- Prioritize regularly backing up your data and testing your backups.

- Prioritize configuring your tablets and laptops to enable full-disk encryption to protect data.

- Communicate to your staff how to recognize common attacks, report attacks or suspicious activity, and perform basic cyber hygiene tasks.

- Detect:

  - Assess your computing technologies and external services for deviations from expected or typical behavior.

  - Prioritize engaging a service provider to monitor computers and networks for suspicious activity if you don't have the resources to do it internally.

- Respond:

  - Understand what your incident response plan is and who has authority and responsibility for implementing various aspects of the plan.

  - Prioritize taking steps to contain and eradicate the incident to prevent further damage.

- Recover:

  - Understand who within and outside your business has recovery responsibilities.

  - Prioritize your recovery actions based on organizational needs, resources, and assets impacted.

This updated guidance from NIST that aligns small businesses to Cybersecurity Framework (CSF) has some excellent resources and guidance for this business size. It speaks in plain business English and provides specific steps business owners and operators can take to reduce their cybersecurity risk. In particular, there are specific recommendations related to IAM and PAM that the business can take to be successful.

Assessment and Risk-Based Approach

We've provided some ways that an organization can assess their current state of PAM: either using NIST-CSF 2.0, the NIST Small Business Guidance, or using the mapping from NIST to match to ISO or another framework. Whether the business is a multinational or a two-person "mom and pop" store, the assessment against the framework chosen will produce three items:

- Current State: What is the current maturity of each of the controls and/or guidance from the framework.

- Target State: What is the maturity level the organization wants to accomplish for each control. In business language, this is what improvements need to be made to the control or guidance to get it where it needs to be to sufficiently lower the cybersecurity risk (this is sometimes referred to as a gap analysis).

- Risk Ranking: The list of current and target state in risk ranking order. From highest to lowest, the list of items to improve helps focus the team on what to do first vs. last.

Critical, High, Medium, and Low

Most organizations still use the qualitative approach to how cybersecurity risk is categorized: critical, high, medium, and low. In order to get this risk rating, the organization must have an enterprise-wide approach on how risk is assessed. There are a number of recommendation on how to do this from standards organizations. NIST provides a Risk Management Framework to assist with this if an organization is looking for guidance. It has a seven-step process to manage risk. It is aligned to NIST 800-53 but can be leveraged without that framework by finding the similar categories in the framework your organization has selected.

One of the most appropriate sites for risk ratings and management is the NIST RMF Quick-Start Guide "Assess Step."[11] From this webpage, there is a link to a PDF that provides excellent guidance on how to select the team, assessment planning, reporting, and remediation steps. It also includes a good section on developing a plan of action and milestones to ensure remediation is tracked and completed.

The challenge the authors view with this approach is primarily around two issues: first is that when looking at quality (qualitative) is it can be viewed as "subjective" to the viewer about what is high vs. low risk. High risk compared to "what" is an often-asked question. The second challenge is very few organizations go back to determine if their risk ranking (critical, high, medium, or low) for the risk was correct. Was the risk really a high, after the project or issue was remediated, or did it actually prove to be a lower level risk to the enterprise? That question is not often asked, and so there is no feedback loop on whether the risk rankings are being done correctly.

---

[11] https://csrc.nist.gov/Projects/risk-management/about-rmf/assess-step

Quantitative Approach

In contrast to the qualitative, the quantitative approach involves math. Math is hard, especially when calculating risk. Risk is the defined as a situation where someone or something is exposed to danger, harm, or loss. It isn't an actual "danger, harm, or loss," so the actual damage cannot be calculated; we are asked to mathematically calculate the probability of it happening along with the damage it will cause (usually financially).

Authors' Note: Why discuss probability in the quantitative approach. As the team does a quantitative assessment of risk, they are determining the probability some bad event will occur. They are not calculating the possibility some bad event will happen. For example, is it possible a bear will come into my home and maul the authors? Yes, it is possible. Is it probable? No, it is not probable because we live in a city that does not have an active bear population for hundreds of miles. The team needs to understand that distinction when performing the calculations and can often be the most challenging integer in the risk rating.

There are a few methods out there that have programs and sales teams around them for doing quantitative risk analysis. Each has its pros and cons, and the authors' role is not to endorse or say one is not good, but like a framework: pick a method, back up why you picked with good business logic, stick with it, and review it periodically for soundness. Whether you pick a commercial solution or do simple "back of the napkin" calculations for damage analysis and probability, describe in the policy and other documentation the reasoning for selecting this method. Then, continue using that method for all other risk assessments, and at least once a year, review that method to see if it is producing the results and outcomes your organization expects.

Quantitative approaches can be better than qualitative because they produce clearer information on relative risk. When performing this type of assessment, the outcomes are almost always in dollar amounts with the level of probability of occurrence (in a certain time frame).

For example, there is a 5% chance of a ransomware attack on our organization in the next three years that will have an impact of $1.5 million. When organizations are looking to rank their risks in priority order, having this level of impact information can make that exercise infinitely easier. As stated above, in qualitative, the list will have a bunch of rankings at the same level: critical, high, medium, or low. How does the team decide which of the 15 high risks is the highest of them vs. the lowest of the bunch? A dollar figure makes sorting much easier.

However, similar to previous advice, the authors recommend picking a method, document why it was picked, stick with that method, and then review that decision on an annual basis.

Zero Trust Journey Assessment

Assessing an organization's progress on a Zero Trust journey is possible thanks to the Cybersecurity and Infrastructure Security Agency (CISA). In April 2023, that organization published version 2.0 of the "Zero Trust Maturity Model[12]" that gives clear guidance on how this can be accomplished.

CISA Guidance

The guidance is in business language and so does not require the reader to have a cybersecurity certification to consume it. There are four levels of maturity described:

- Traditional

- Initial

---

[12] https://www.cisa.gov/sites/default/files/2023-04/zero_trust_maturity_model_v2_508.pdf

- Advanced

- Optimal

There are five pillars in the model:

- Identity

- Devices

- Networks

- Applications and workloads

- Data

The publication has an excellent table that describes what to expect in each of the pillars for maturity decisions.

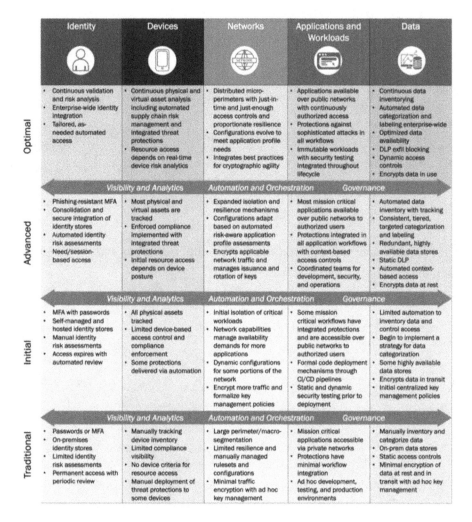

Figure 3-7. *High-Level Zero Trust Maturity Model Overview*

This document along with other resources provided by CISA will provide enough detail about how to assess an organization's Zero Trust maturity; it also provides some excellent potential maturity goals so enterprises can lay out a strategy and road map.

Chapter Summary

In this chapter, we discussed

- Strategy, Again: It is not enough to list risks; there needs to be a goal or strategy to guide the team to success.

- Importance of Frameworks: A short discussion of why frameworks are important to the success of cybersecurity.

- Current State: We discussed a number of ways to assess an organization's current PAM maturity.

- Assessment and Risk-Based Approach: Taking a risk-based approach is crucial to success as well as having a solid program and project management oversight.

- Zero Trust Journey Assessment: We discussed some great tools on how to assess a Zero Trust journey that can be leveraged.

CHAPTER 4

PAM Governance

Chapter Overview

In this chapter, we will discuss the following:

- Case Studies: Overview of what is involved in making a product PAM environment ready.

- Small and Medium Businesses: Provide a detailed example of successful PAM implementations in the smallest organizations.

- Small and Medium Enterprises: Provide a detailed example of different PAM implementations in these medium-sized companies.

- Large Enterprises: Explain how the largest organizations can accomplish PAM implementations.

Case Studies

In this chapter section, we want to provide the reader with some ways Privileged Access Management was deployed at different organizations based on size and complexity. There are several standards or directives across the world on how to measure business size. We've chosen

© Gregory C. Rasner, Maria C. Rasner 2025
G. C. Rasner and M. C. Rasner, *Privileged Access Management*,
https://doi.org/10.1007/979-8-8688-1431-0_4

three basic "buckets" to help readers place their organization into the appropriate slot for comparison. The buckets are Small and Medium Businesses (SMB), Small and Medium Enterprises (SME), and Large Enterprises (LE). We will explain how each of these categories is determined and then provide hands-on examples of what a best-practice PAM program would contain and have as strategy and outcomes.

Policy, Standard, Procedures, and Guidelines: What's the difference

The need to write, publish, and disseminate documentation in any organization depends on the size. As will be discussed in the next few pages, the amount of people and revenue (along with risk) will determine the amount of documentation and how much effort is put into communicating it. However, the principles are the same regardless of the size and complexity. And taxonomy matters, so to be sure everyone is on the same page, let's define and discuss each of the types of common governance documents.

Policy

A policy is a top-level document that sets out expectations and general management statements to the organization. One of the best purposes these can be used for is to explain the "why" things are the way they are. Why do we require more than 12 characters in our passwords, or why does the organization require a certain level of protection for classified assets and resources. When a user or group is curious why something is done the way it is or if there is a risk based upon their work observations, send them to the policy-level documentation.

Standards

A standard is a set of prescribed practice around a technology, product, category, or service. These documents are designed to address the "when" and the "what" (in comparison to the "why" in the policy). For example, a standard would be utilized for a user when they want to know when to do a certain action or reaction. A standard can also provide the what in the action or reaction involved. A standard document can provide system administrators with descriptions of how to install a new server and steps to complete it per the "standard."

Procedures

Procedures, which can include things like runbooks or playbooks, are designed to provide the very specific "how" part of the question. Procedures are often step-by-step guides on who and how to perform a set of actions for a set outcome. For example, there could be a runbook for how backups are performed or actions to take in the event of a breach.

The way to think of the value of this documentation is it is critical for daily success and long-term strategy as well. If an activity isn't written down, step-by-step, then it will be done differently every, single, time. Guaranteed. If an activity isn't written down, then there is no way to validate it is being done correctly by everyone. When an activity isn't written down, there is very little chance for improvement. Lastly, let's be positive about why this is important: when you leave this job or role (whether you win the lottery or get promoted or find your next dream job), it is being a good professional to leave documentation for the next person to pick up the job with little difficulty.

Author's Aside: Documentation Matters

A personal anecdotal story from one of the authors (we will leave both the author and company nameless to protect the innocent) to illustrate the importance of written policies, standards, and procedures. At a company in which they were an IT leader, one of the system administrators would sometimes complain about the need to write runbooks or consult a policy document. Fast forward a few months later, and the author has left the company, and that organization gets bought by a larger firm. The author gets a frantic call from the same system administrator who suddenly understood why documentation was so important. The larger company didn't have any proper standards or runbooks, and so, this was causing all kinds of outages and events because of this lack of discipline.

Documentation takes a bit of investment in time up front, and that can sometimes feel like it intrudes on your execution time. However, make that time to document it, review it, publish it, and communicate it out. Long term, it will provide much smoother sailing for operations and improvements.

Guidelines

A guideline can be thought of as a recommendation (or a set of recommendations). A guideline in a technology organization might be a guideline published on how to send email securely or to avoid a phishing scam. Guidelines are not meant to be enforced through actions but are designed to help users with making better-informed decisions.

Align Policy with Framework

As we discuss the rest of this chapter, there will be discussion and expansion on best practices and policy. As described in an earlier chapter, a policy or standard must align to a framework to be complete and valid. If it isn't tied to a framework, it can be thought of as a "bucket of best practices." It might be a great policy, but without the connection to a framework, it is likely going to miss a control or two (or more). Also, it is challenging to update since there is no way to find out what might be missing, since the lack of connection to a framework means updates must be done by manual search.

NIST-CSF Policy Template Guide

One of the best ways to determine if your policies align with your framework is published by the Center For Internet Security: NIST Cybersecurity Framework, Policy Template Guide.[1] This document breaks down by NIST function what policies are appropriate and even provides some sample documents. For the purpose of this book, we will only focus on those areas in NIST-CSF and documentation that are IAM and PAM related. As your organization looks to create or update documentation, this policy template guide is a great starting point. If your organization uses ISO 27000 series or another framework, there are guides that provide a "translation" from NIST-CSF to almost every other known framework.

NIST SB Guidance

The National Institute of Standards and Technology (NIST) has published a very good guide for businesses of this size (and slightly larger) on cybersecurity. This was published in 2016 and is still largely relevant as it covers the "basics" for this business size. It starts the first section describing why it was written and other introductory information. Section 2 provides information on how to implement a security program at a small business. Section 3 discusses key steps small businesses can take to develop or improve their information security and data security. Section

---

[1] https://www.cisecurity.org/-/jssmedia/Project/cisecurity/cisecurity/data/media/img/uploads/2021/11/NIST-Cybersecurity-Framework-Policy-Template-Guide-v2111Online.pdf

4 provides several key practices that entrepreneurs can take immediately to lower their risk of an event, incident, or a breach. The pleasant thing to report is the publication is fairly short at only 32 pages by the end of Section 4. Another key piece of information in this document is Appendix D, which contains a few worksheets that professionals will find useful.

Regarding the issue of privileged user controls, like Privileged Access Management (PAM), it is covered in Section 3.1 (Identify), under "*Identify and control who has access to your business information.*"[2] In this section, the reader is requested to determine who has or should have access to their organization's data or technology and then determine whether they require a "key, administrative privilege, or password." Put more simply, as a small business owner, take an inventory of all your sensitive data and technology. Determine who has access to that data, both physically and logically. We often think of the logical access, where someone logs in over their computer, but we often forget the physical access issues or risks. Physically, in terms of who can get to be able (or should be able) to touch or come in contact with data (think of paper records) or the technology that stores that data.

Next, in the same Section 3.1 (Identify), under the heading "Require individual user accounts for each employee."[3] This requires what is considered best practices to not have shared accounts but to ensure each user gets their own login. It recommends ensuring "normal" employees who have computer accounts are not privileged to avoid installation of malware or unauthorized software.

In Section 3.2 (Protect), it provides some best practices on changing the administrator's password on any firewall or other similar network devices. The word it uses is "consider" which is not strong enough: best practice is to immediately change the default passwords, and in fact, good software or hardware will force a change in default passwords. This is "built-in security."

---

[2] https://nvlpubs.nist.gov/nistpubs/ir/2016/nist.ir.7621r1.pdf
[3] https://nvlpubs.nist.gov/nistpubs/ir/2016/nist.ir.7621r1.pdf

In Section E, the document provides some excellent examples of how to write policies and procedures. The example they provide is right within where our book is focused, on identity and administrators:

Example procedure supporting a policy:

Policy: All computer users will have their own account and password.

Procedure:

1. *Supervisor completes/signs account creation request form for new user and sends it to the system administrator [Note that the account request form would be part of the procedure];*

2. *System administrator creates new account with unique identifier;*

3. *System administrator assigns a temporary password to new account;*

4. *System administrator notifies the new user of the unique account identifier and temporary password;*

5. *New user logs into the new account and is prompted to immediately change the password;*

6. *System administrator reviews user accounts monthly.[4]*

The authors of this book highly recommend this NIST publication for any small business of 1 to 200 or even slightly more employees. It provides a good primer on cybersecurity for those who are not experts; it is short enough not to bore the reader to death but includes what is really critical for this type of small business, and it provides some great examples and templates for the user to get started and avoid having to "create the wheel."

---

[4]https://nvlpubs.nist.gov/nistpubs/ir/2016/nist.ir.7621r1.pdf

Small and Medium Businesses

In this tier, we have nearly all the businesses (99%) in the United States.[5] The characteristics of this type of business are under 100 for small business and 100 to 1,000 for medium business. Revenue in this category is under $50 million for small businesses and under $500 million for medium businesses. The vast majority of the businesses in this category are one- or two-person shops (at most), and these can be the biggest challenge.

The typical types of businesses in this category run from sole proprietorships like consultants, tax advisors, small shop owners, independent contractors, professional tradespeople, etc. Many of the companies in this space have one or two professional IT people at the most. However, for the sole proprietorships, the owner/operator is the IT support. A lawyer, a tax accountant, a barber, and others are great at what they do, but that will not make them excellent at IT and cybersecurity.

Let us state that many of these small businesses would benefit from engaging with a Managed Service Security Provider (MSSP) or MSP (Managed Service Provider) to alleviate the risk and time sink these activities can become. There are a large number of options and price ranges out there. As always, do the due diligence and due care for any engagement with a vendor, especially one you're going to entrust with such an important and risk function.

---

[5] U.S. Small Business Administration 2021 Census

A Lesson for SMBs and Cost of a Breach: Insolvency

In 2023, National Public Data, a Florida-based data broker that does background checks, was hacked.[6] This company was run by a one person (presumably the owner and founder) out of their home in Pompano Beach, Florida. The company provided background checks for a large number of Fortune 500 companies and as a result had 2.9 billion records that included social security numbers and home addresses. It was a gold mine for hackers. The lack of a cyber strategy, perhaps even awareness of the cyber risk, added to the lack of documented controls and procedures was the most likely cause of this breach.

The lesson for other small business owners is that National Public Data's parent company, Jericho Pictures, filed for Chapter 11 bankruptcy protection. The reason for these cash flow issues was a result of the regulatory investigations, prosecutorial pursuit by attorney's generals, lawsuits, and requirements for consumer notification that were more than what the company could absorb. There are other similar examples in the wild of how a lack of understanding of the risk by small business owners and operators has cost them everything they worked so hard to create.

People

This is truly a "small business" with only one to four people, often involving family members or close friends. By definition, this is a small shop, and there is no division of labor or limited ability to have one person check the actions of another given the small size. As the wearer of many hats, the owner of this business is doing everything: building the business

---

[6] https://www.wsj.com/articles/for-some-companies-the-real-cost-of-a-cyberattack-is-telling-everyone-about-it-735bee74?tpl=cs&mod=hp_lead_pos3

and securing it. The amount of documentation created here is minimal and mostly designed to promote best practice by the owner/operator and to provide any prospective customer with assurances the organization has some governance.

For a medium business, there is a good reason to expect to have one to three professionals working on information technology and security. The expectation would be they are creating some documentation as described in the Process section. The documentation would include a few runbooks and playbooks, along with some top-level policy and standards documents to be tied to a framework.

SMBs are also great candidates to get some outside help. In the later business size (Small and Medium Enterprise, SME), we discuss Managed Service Providers (MSP) and Managed Security Service Providers (MSSP) that can assist in this space. The complexity and velocity of cyber and information technology challenges means it is recommended to enlist help from experts. Luckily, there has been an explosion of these MSP and MSSP firms in the last 10 years which provide a lot of options for either project-, point-, or subscription-based solutions for SMBs and SMEs. If this is of interest to your team, skip down to that section a few pages down.

Process

In the governance and process of the Small and Medium Business, there is a need for documentation, but it can be light due to the nature and size of the business. As discussed and suggested, the aim would be to leverage NIST's Small Business guidance to develop and publish the policies, standards, procedures, and guidelines. The major benefit in developing this documentation for an SMB is primarily two big reasons:

> Regulators: Whether you're a barber shop, nail
> salon, law office, or any other number of the types of
> businesses in this category, don't fool yourself and

assume you are not regulated. There are numerous privacy laws in many US states, for example, that your business would be held to in the event of a breach of the customer database. Having this important governance documentation written down can mean a huge difference between a slap on the wrist (figuratively) vs. a hefty fine because the regulator finds you negligent.

Repeatable Process: This is listed second, but it is really the most important factor in developing governance documentation. Even for an SMB. As an owner or member of an SMB, the daily work of running this enterprise can consume the whole day and your mind, making critical decisions on topics you are not always familiar with a potential pitfall. For example, let's assume you are running a law office as a single attorney. You are great as an attorney, getting clients and defending their best interests in whatever capacity you've been hired to complete.

However, you are not a cyber or information technology expert, and how you design or implement multifactor authentication is not "top-of-mind." The lawyer knows the law like the back of their hand, but IT and cyber support is not their main business objective. Having this important items written down enables you to figure out how to do something important (and potentially mundane even) that is not your day-to-day activity. It requires that it be written down to ensure the process is repeated correctly. Another analogy that might hit home: it is the reason we (as humans) write down recipes on how to make a cake or bread, to ensure it is done correctly every single time.

Policy

Policies in this size of a business can be fairly light and focused on the items that really matter to ensure a safe and stable technology environment at the SMB. Leveraging the NIST Small Business Quick-Start Guide,[7] we can go through the sections provided to develop the policies needed for this type and size of business. Below are some templates for these organizations to leverage, and the expectation is there may be some customization due to needs and circumstances.

The authors have used a number of resources to develop these policy documents; much of it from previous experience. The NIST Cybersecurity Framework Policy Template Guide v. 2.1 is an excellent resource for those starting out or looking to tie their policies and standards back to a framework.

Below are the policies that would be most critical to have as an SMB relevant to this book: Information Technology and Security Policy, Privacy Policy, and an Identity and Access Management Policy (which at this size of a company includes Remote Access Policies, Account Management Policies, Access Control Policies, Password Protection Policies, and Database Credentials Policies that are typically separate documents in larger organizations).

Information Technology (IT) and Security Policy

This is a top-level policy that is the best starting point and one of the most valuable. This policy is designed to inform yourself, employees, and partners what the standards they have to adhere to when using technology in your business. The IT policy is designed to inform expectations on use and behavior as well as consequences for failure to adhere to these expectations. Typically, the policy will provide guidance on the following topics:

---

[7] https://nvlpubs.nist.gov/nistpubs/SpecialPublications/NIST.SP.1300.pdf

- Internet use

- Social media

- Email

- Mobile device use

- Other business equipment use

- Ability of SMB to monitor use

(SMB Name) Information Technology and Security Policy

About

This policy sets forth the Company's guidelines regarding the use of and access to its computer systems, including the Internet and email. This policy always applies, regardless of location. The use of IT resources and surveillance is emphasized. Any email use, Internet use, or voice content must not be detrimental to, nor adversely affect, the reputation or operations of the Company, its employees, or customers. Employees are responsible and accountable for their email use, Internet use, and voice communications, including the content of these. Any social media use in a personal capacity must also not be detrimental to, nor adversely affect, the reputation or operations of the Company, its employees, or customers. You must not present or communicate on behalf of the Company on social media without the prior authorization of the Company.

Any social media use in a work or personal capacity must comply with this policy. All access to and usage of the Company's data, or any email or voice communications using company equipment or resources, may be monitored or accessed by authorized employees. The Company also reserves the right to monitor, access, and record Internet usage and web browsing activity of all employees in the workplace or using company resources.

General Use

At all times, you must also comply with the following: You may use the Company's IT resources for business purposes and reasonable personal use, provided that such use does not bring the Company or its related entities into disrepute and is not contrary to this policy or any applicable law. Personal use must be kept to a minimum, not preventing you from properly performing your duties; you must not use any of the Company's property or IT resources to deal with illegal, offensive, or defamatory material, including creating, downloading, transmitting, forwarding, copying, or saving such material; you must not use the Company's property or IT resources to act in a manner inconsistent with this policy. If any questions or doubts about an activity need to be corrected, it is the responsibility of the employee or partner to request clarification.

Internet Use Guidelines

(SMB Name) recognizes that the Internet is an integral part of business. Therefore, it encourages its employees to use the Internet whenever such use supports the company's goals and objectives. For instance, employees members may use the Internet to perform normal business operations, such as purchasing office supplies, booking business-related travel, or researching competitors, suppliers, or customers. There are many valid reasons for using the Internet at work, and the company allows its employees to explore and leverage the Internet for business-related needs.

Personal Internet Use

The company also recognizes that the Internet is integral to many people's daily lives. As such, it allows employees to use the Internet for personal reasons, with the following stipulations:

Personal Internet use should be reasonable and restricted to nonwork times, such as breaks and lunch. All rules described in this policy apply equally to personal Internet use. For instance, inappropriate content is always inappropriate, regardless of whether it is being accessed for business or personal reasons. Personal Internet use must not affect the

Internet service available to other people in the company. For instance, downloading large files could slow access for all employees.

Authorized Users

Only people authorized to use the Internet at (SMB Name) may do so. Authorization is usually provided by an employee's manager. It is typically granted when a new employee joins the company and is assigned login details for its IT systems.

Email Use

Business Email Use

(SMB name) acknowledges that email is a key communication tool. It encourages its employees to use email whenever appropriate. For instance, employees members may use email to

- Communicate with customers or suppliers

- Market the company's products

- Distribute information to colleagues

- Personal use of email

The company also recognizes that email is an important tool in many people's daily lives. As such, it allows employees to use their company email account for personal reasons, with the following conditions:

Personal email use should be of a reasonable level and restricted to nonwork times, such as breaks and during lunch.

All rules described in this policy apply equally to personal email use. For instance, inappropriate content is always inappropriate, no matter whether it is being sent or received for business or personal reasons.

Personal email use must not affect the email service available to other users. For instance, sending exceptionally large files by email could slow access for other employees.

Users may access their own personal email accounts at work, if they can do so via our Internet connection. For instance, an employees member may check their mail during their break.

Email Security

Used inappropriately, email can be a source of security problems for the company. Users of the company email system must not

- Open email attachments from unknown sources, in case they contain a virus, Trojan, spyware, or other malware.

- Disable security or email scanning software. These tools are essential to protect the business from security problems.

- Send confidential company data via email. The IT department can advise on appropriate tools to use instead.

- Access another user's company email account. If they require access to a specific message (for instance, while an employee is off sick), they should approach their line manager or the IT department.

Employees must always consider the security of the company's systems and data when using email. If required, help and guidance is available from line managers and the company IT department. Users should note that email is not inherently secure. Most emails transmitted over the Internet are sent in plain text. This means they are vulnerable to interception. Although such interceptions are rare, it's best to regard email as an open communication system, not suitable for confidential messages and information. Inappropriate email content and the company email system must not be used to send or store inappropriate content or materials. It is important employees understand that viewing or distributing inappropriate content via email is not acceptable under any circumstances. Users will not

- Write or send emails that might be defamatory or incur liability for the company.

- Create or distribute any inappropriate content or material via email.

- Inappropriate content includes pornography, racial or religious slurs, gender-specific comments, information encouraging criminal skills or terrorism, or materials relating to cults, gambling, and illegal drugs.

- This definition of inappropriate content or material also covers any text, images, or other media that could reasonably offend someone on the

- basis of race, age, sex, religious or political beliefs, national origin, disability, sexual orientation, or any other characteristic protected by law.

- Use email for any illegal or criminal activities.

- Send offensive or harassing emails to others.

- Send messages or material that could damage (SMB name)'s image or reputation. Any user who receives an email they consider to be inappropriate should report this to their manager.

Social Media Policy

Everyone who operates a company social media account or uses their personal social media accounts at work has some responsibility for implementing this policy. However, these people have key responsibilities:

- The manager is ultimately responsible for ensuring that (SMB name) uses social media safely, appropriately, and in line with the company's objectives.

- The manager is responsible for providing apps and tools to manage the company's social media presence and track key performance indicators. They are also responsible for proactively monitoring social media security threats.

- The manager is responsible for working with the social media owner to roll out marketing ideas and campaigns through our social media channels.

- The manager is responsible for following up on social media requests for assistance and support. Here are general social media guidelines.

The Value and Power of Social Media

(SMB name) recognizes that social media offers a platform for the company to perform marketing, stay connected with customers, and build its profile online. The company also believes its employees should be involved in industry conversations on social networks. Social media is an excellent way for employees to make valuable connections, share ideas, and shape discussions. The company, therefore, encourages employees to use social media to support the company's goals and objectives. Regardless of which social networks employees are using or whether they're using business or personal accounts on company time, it is essential to follow these simple rules, which help avoid the most common pitfalls: Know the social network. Employees should spend time becoming familiar with the social network before contributing. It's essential to read any FAQs and understand what is and is not acceptable on a network before posting messages or updates.

If unsure, don't post it. Employees should be cautious when posting to social networks. If an employee feels an update or message might cause complaints or offenses—or be unsuitable—they should not post it. Employees members can always consult their manager for advice.

Be thoughtful and polite.

Many social media users have gotten into trouble simply by failing to observe good manners online. Employees should adopt the same level of courtesy used when communicating via email. Look out for security threats. Employees and other members should guard against social engineering and phishing attempts. Social networks are also used to distribute spam and malware. Further details are below.

Keep personal use reasonable.

Although the company believes that having active employees on social media can be valuable both to those employees and to the business, employees should exercise restraint in how much personal use of social media they make during working hours.

Don't make promises without checking.

Some social networks are very public, so employees should not make any commitments or promises on behalf of (SMB name) without checking that the company can deliver on those promises. Direct any inquiries to the [social media manager]. Handle complex queries via other channels. Social networks are not a good place to resolve complicated inquiries and customer issues. Once a customer has contacted, employees should handle further communications via the most appropriate channel—email or telephone. Don't escalate things. It's easy to post a quick response to a contentious status update and then regret it. Employees should always take the time to think before responding and hold back if they are in doubt.

Inappropriate Content

Company social media accounts must not be used to share or spread inappropriate content or participate in any activities that could bring the company into disrepute. When sharing an exciting blog post, article, or piece of content, employees should always review the content thoroughly and not post a link based solely on a headline.

157

Personal Social Media Rules

Acceptable use

- Employees may use their personal social media accounts for work-related purposes during regular hours but must ensure this is for a specific reason (e.g., competitor research). Social media should not affect the ability of employees to perform their regular duties.

- Use of social media accounts for nonwork purposes is restricted to nonwork times, such as breaks and during lunch. Talking about the company:

- Employees should ensure their social media account does not represent [company name]'s views or opinions.

- Employees may wish to include a disclaimer in social media profiles: "The views expressed are my own and do not reflect the views of my employer."

The rules in this section apply to

- Any employees using company social media accounts

- Employees using personal social media accounts during company time must not

- Create or transmit material that might be defamatory or incur liability for the company.

  - Post messages, status updates, or links to inappropriate material or content. Inappropriate content includes pornography, racial or religious slurs, gender-specific comments, information encouraging criminal skills or terrorism, or materials relating to cults, gambling, and illegal drugs. This definition of inappropriate content or material also covers any text, images, or other media that could reasonably offend someone based on race, age, sex, religious or political beliefs, national origin, disability, sexual orientation, or any other characteristic protected by law.

- Use social media for any illegal or criminal activities.

- Send offensive or harassing material to others via social media.

- Broadcast unsolicited views on social, political, religious, or other non-business-related matters.

- Send or post messages or material that could damage [company name]'s image or reputation.

- Interact with [company name]'s competitors in any way that could be interpreted as offensive, disrespectful, or rude. (Communication with direct competitors should be kept to a minimum.)

- Discuss colleagues, competitors, customers, or suppliers without their approval.

- Post, upload, forward, or link to spam, junk email, or chain emails and messages.

Security and Data Protection

Employees should be aware of the security and data protection issues arising from using social networks.

Confidentiality

Users must not

- Share or link to any content or information the company owns that could be considered confidential or commercially sensitive. This might include sales figures, details of key customers, or information about future strategy or marketing campaigns.

- Share or link to any content or data owned by another company or person that could be considered confidential or commercially sensitive. For example, if a competitor's marketing strategy was leaked online, employees of (SMB name) should not mention it on social media.

- Share or link to data in any way that could breach the company's data protection policy.

Protect Social Media Accounts

- Company social media accounts should be protected by strong passwords that are changed regularly and shared only with authorized users.

- Wherever possible, employees should use two-factor authentication (often called mobile phone verification) to safeguard company accounts.

- Employees must not use any new software, app, or service with any of the company's social media accounts without receiving approval from the manager.

Avoid Social Scams

Employees should watch for phishing attempts, where scammers may use deception to obtain information relating to either the company or its customers. Employees should never reveal sensitive details through social media channels. Customer identities must always be verified in the usual way before any account information is shared or discussed.

Employees should avoid clicking links in posts, updates, and direct messages that look suspicious. In particular, users should look for URLs in generic or vague-sounding direct messages.

Policy Enforcement

Monitoring social media use. Company IT and Internet resources—including computers, smartphones, and Internet connections—are provided for legitimate business use. The company reserves the right to monitor how social networks are used and accessed through these resources. Any such examinations or monitoring will only be carried out by authorized employees.

Additionally, all data relating to social networks written, sent, or received through the company's computer systems is part of official (SMB name) records. The company can be legally compelled to demonstrate that information to law enforcement agencies or other parties.

Potential Sanctions

Knowingly breaching this social media policy is a serious matter. Users who do so will be subject to disciplinary action, up to and including termination of employment. Employees, contractors, and other users may also be held personally liable for violating this policy. Where appropriate, the company will involve the police or other law enforcement agencies about breaches of this policy.

Updates and Version Control

This policy will be reviewed annually for any changes due to regulatory or environmental factors.

Version Control Table

Version Number	Purpose/Change	Author	Date

(SMB Name) Privacy Policy

At (SMB Name), safeguarding your privacy and information security is our foremost commitment. We are devoted to ensuring the confidentiality of the data you provide and employing strong cybersecurity measures to thwart unauthorized access.

Privacy Promise

We understand that our relationship with you relies on trust, and we are dedicated to conducting business that justifies that trust. Any nonpublic personal information you share is handled with utmost confidentiality. Regardless of whether you are an active client or have closed your accounts, we follow the privacy policies and practices detailed here.

How and Why We Collect Sensitive Information

(SMB Name) can gather "nonpublic personal information" to offer you customized financial services and solutions. This data might include your name, Social Security number, assets, income, account activity, and other information obtained from applications, transactions, or online interactions with us.

How We Protect Sensitive Data

(SMB Name) employs a combination of physical, electronic, and procedural safeguards that meet federal standards to protect your nonpublic personal information. We enforce strict confidentiality policies among our employees and strategic partners, ensuring that access to your information is restricted to those who require it to provide services. Furthermore, we will only share your information with affiliates or third parties as mandated by law or necessary for service support, such as financial institutions or service providers who are bound by confidentiality agreements.

How We Maintain Confidentiality

We do not share any private personal information about our current or former clients, except as allowed by law. Access to your data is limited to employees or strategic partners who require it for service delivery. We will not distribute your information to external entities unless previously communicated to you, authorized by you, or permitted by law. Any medical information, if collected, will only be used for insurance underwriting or as otherwise authorized.

Cybersecurity Controls

To protect your information, we implement data encryption, access controls, secure network connections, and conduct regular system monitoring. Our network undergoes 24/7 surveillance, and we enforce strong password policies along with two-factor authentication for accessing sensitive data.

Shared Responsibility

This is a team effort. We implement strict cybersecurity practices but also advise clients to adopt robust online security habits, such as creating strong passwords and being alert to phishing attempts. Although no system can provide total security, we can collaboratively work to reduce risks. If you have any questions or concerns regarding your information's security or privacy, please refer to the privacy statement on our website, which is updated as necessary to meet environmental or regulatory standards.

Updates and Version Control

This policy will be reviewed annually for any changes due to regulatory or environmental factors.

Version Control Table

Version Number	Purpose/Change	Author	Date

SMB Identity and Access Management (IAM) Policy

Remote Access Policies, Account Management Policies, Access Control Policies, Password Protection Policies, and Database Credentials Policies

Account Management

Overview

Computer accounts serve as access points to (SMB Name)'s information systems. They play a crucial role in ensuring accountability, which is fundamental to any computer security program at (SMB Name). Therefore, it is essential to create, manage, and monitor all computer accounts as part of a comprehensive security strategy.

Purpose

This policy aims to set a standard for creating, managing, using, and removing accounts that provide access to information and technology resources at (SMB Name).

Audience

This policy is applicable to employees, volunteers, contractors, consultants, temporary workers, and others associated with (SMB Name), as well as all third-party personnel with authorized access to any information systems of (SMB Name).

Accounts

- Every account created requires a written request and signed management approval suitable for the (SMB Name) system or service.

- Each account needs to be distinctly identifiable with the assigned username.

- Shared accounts within (SMB Name) information systems are prohibited.

- Refer to the Employee Access During Leave of Absence Policy for guidance on removing an employee's access during their leave of absence or vacation.

- All default account passwords must be created following the (SMB Name) Password Policy.

- Every account must adhere to the password expiration requirements set out in the (SMB Name) Password Policy.

- Concurrent connections may be restricted for technical or security reasons.

- All accounts must be disabled immediately following any notification of an employee's termination.

The following items apply to all employees and any staff:

- User accounts within the information system must be set up to enforce the strictest rights, privileges, or access necessary for individual task performance.

- Additionally, to prevent conflicts of interest, no user should have the ability to authorize, perform, review, and audit a single transaction.

- All information system accounts will undergo active management, which entails establishing, activating, modifying, disabling, and removing accounts as required.

- Access controls will be defined according to established procedures for onboarding new employees, handling employee transitions, processing terminations, and managing leaves of absence.

- All changes to user accounts need a documented procedure, especially for name or permission updates..

- Information system accounts are to be reviewed monthly to identify inactive accounts. If an employee or third-party account is inactive for 30 days, the owners (of the account) and their manager will be notified of pending disablement. If the account remains inactive for 15 days, it will be manually disabled.

- A list of accounts for the systems they administer must be provided when requested by authorized (SMB Name) management.

- An independent audit review may be performed to ensure the accounts are correctly managed.

Password Policies and Rules

Overview

Passwords are crucial in computer security, serving as the primary defense for user accounts. A weak password could lead to a breach of (SMB Name)'s entire corporate network. Therefore, all employees, volunteers, directors, contractors, and vendors with access to (SMB Name) systems must take the measures outlined below to choose and protect their passwords.

Purpose

This policy establishes guidelines for creating strong passwords, protecting them, and defining their update frequency. It applies to all staff, volunteers, and anyone who holds or manages an account—or has any access requiring a password—on any system within a (SMB Name) facility, connected to the (SMB Name) network, or storing any confidential (SMB Name) information.

User Passwords

- For access to the (SMB Name) network, passwords should follow these guidelines:

  - Change passwords every 90 days.

  - Ensure passwords are at least ten characters long.

  - Include a mix of letters, numbers, and special characters, as allowed by the computing system. (!@#$%^&*_+=?/~';'<>|\).

- Passwords must not be easily tied back to the account owner such as

  - Username, Social Security number, nickname, relative's name, birth date, etc.

- Passwords must not be dictionary words or acronyms.

- Passwords cannot be reused for one year.

System-Level Passwords

- All system-level passwords must follow these guidelines:

  - Passwords should be changed at least every six months.

  - All administrator accounts require 12-character passwords, which must include three of the following four criteria: upper case letters, lower case letters, numbers, and special characters.

  - Documentation must be provided for non-expiring passwords, outlining the requirements for those accounts, which must comply with the same standards as administrator accounts.

  - Administrators are prohibited from bypassing the Password Policy for convenience.

Password Protection

- Do not reuse the same password across different accounts.

- Passwords should remain confidential and not be shared with anyone.

- Treat all passwords as sensitive information belonging to (SMB Name).

167

- Ensure that stored passwords are encrypted.

- Avoid including passwords in emails or electronic messages. Do not divulge passwords over the phone.

- Never disclose passwords in questionnaires or security forms.

- Users must not provide clues about password formats, such as hinting with phrases like "my family name."

- While on vacation, (SMB Name) passwords should not be shared with anyone, including colleagues, supervisors, or family.

- Do not write down passwords or store them anywhere in the office.

- Avoid saving passwords in files on a computer or mobile device (like a phone or tablet) unless they are encrypted.

- If there's a concern about account security, change the password right away. If passwords are found or discovered, take these steps:

  - Gain control of the passwords and secure them.

  - Inform your manager about the discovery.

- Users are not allowed to bypass password entry through auto logon, application memory, embedded scripts, or hard-coded passwords within client software. Exceptions can be granted for certain applications, such as automated backup processes, but only with IT's approval. To gain approval for an exception, a procedure to change the passwords must be established.

- PCs must not be left unattended without enabling a password-protected screensaver or logging off the device.

- If there's a concern about account security, change the password right away. If passwords are found or discovered, take these steps:

  - Gain control of the passwords and secure them.

  - Inform IT about the discovery.

- Security tokens, such as smartcards and RSA hardware tokens, must be returned upon request or when the relationship with (SMB Name) ends.

Database Credentials Policy

Overview

Database authentication credentials are essential for authorizing applications to connect with internal databases. However, improper use, storage, and transmission of these credentials can result in the compromise of highly sensitive assets, potentially leading to broader security breaches within the organization.

General

To ensure the security of (SMB Name)'s internal databases, software programs can only gain access after successful credential authentication. These credentials should not be included in the program's main source code in plain text or in easily reversible encryption. Additionally, database credentials must not be stored in areas accessible via a web server. The algorithms utilized must conform to the standards set by NIST publication FIPS 140-2 or any relevant subsequent documents based on the implementation date. It is strongly recommended to use RSA and Elliptic Curve Cryptography (ECC) algorithms for asymmetric encryption.

Storage of Data Base Usernames and Passwords

Usernames and passwords for the database might be kept in a file that is distinct from the program's executable code. It is crucial that this file is not accessible for anyone to read or write.

Database credentials may also be located on the database server itself. If so, a hash value representing these credentials can be included in the coded section of the program.

Additionally, database credentials might be part of an authentication server, like an LDAP server, which is utilized for user verification. In such instances, the database authentication can be performed on behalf of the program during the user authentication at the server, eliminating the need for the program to directly handle the database credentials. Database credentials may not reside in the documents tree of a web server.

Retrieval of Database User Names and Passwords

If database user names and passwords are stored in a non-source code file, they should be read from it right before use. After database authentication, you must release or clear the memory that held these credentials. Database credentials should be stored in a scope that is physically distinct from other areas of your code; for instance, keep them in a separate source file. This credentials file should include only the user name, password, and any functions, routines, or methods necessary to access these credentials. For languages that execute from source code, the credentials' source file must not reside in the same browsable or executable file directory tree in which the executing body of code resides.

Access to Database Usernames and Passwords

Each program or set of programs performing a specific business function must utilize distinct database credentials. Sharing credentials among programs is prohibited.

Database passwords utilized by programs are classified as system-level passwords following the Password Policy.

Developer teams need a robust process to manage and update database passwords in line with the Password Policy. This procedure should ensure that knowledge of database passwords is limited to individuals on a need-to-know basis.

Users or software accessing sensitive information must implement proper access controls and should be unable to perform privileged actions beyond their assigned scope.

Account Types

Account types include individual, privileged, service, shared, default non-privileged (e.g., guest, anonymous), emergency, and temporary. All account types must adhere to all applicable rules as defined in this policy.

Individual Accounts: An individual account is a unique account issued to a single user. The account enables the user to authenticate to systems with a digital identity. After a user is authenticated, the user is authorized or denied access to the system based on the permissions that are assigned directly or indirectly to that user.

Privileged Accounts: A privileged account is an account which provides increased access and requires additional authorization. Examples include a network, system, or security administrator account. A privileged account may only be provided to members of the workforce who require it to accomplish their job duties. The use of privileged accounts must be compliant with the principle of least privilege. Access will be restricted to only those programs or processes specifically needed to perform authorized business tasks and no more. There are two privileged account types—administrative accounts and default accounts.

Administrative Accounts: Accounts granted to a user that enable modification of the operating system or platform settings or those that permit changes to other accounts. These accounts must

- Maintain an Identity Assurance Level appropriate for the protected resources accessed.

171

- Not possess user IDs that suggest the user's privilege level, such as supervisor, manager, administrator, or similar titles.

- Be identifiable internally as an administrative account following a standardized naming convention.

- Be revoked according to organizational requirements.

Default Privileged Accounts: Default privileged accounts (e.g., root, administrator) are provided with a particular system and cannot be removed without affecting the functionality of the system. Default privileged accounts must

- Be inactive when not in use or renamed if technically feasible.

- It should only be utilized for the initial system installation or as a service account.

- Alerts must be sent to the relevant personnel whenever there is an attempt to log in with this account.

- Avoid using the default password provided with the system.

- The password should be known or accessible to at least two individuals.

Service Accounts: A service account is not intended to be given to a user but is provided for a process. It is to be used in situations such as to allow a system to run jobs and services independent of user interaction. Service accounts must

- Have an assigned owner responsible for documenting and managing the account.

- Be restricted to specific devices and hours when possible.

- Never be used interactively by a user for any purpose other than the initial system installation or if absolutely required for system troubleshooting or maintenance. Wherever technically feasible, administrators should leverage "switch user" (SU) or "run as" for executing processes as service accounts.

- Never be used for any purpose beyond their initial scope.

- Be internally identifiable as a service account per a standardized naming convention, where possible.

- Not allow its password to be reset according to any standardized and/or forced schedule. However, should an employee with knowledge of said password leave the entity, that password must be changed immediately.

- Have the password known or accessible by at least two individuals within the entity, if the password is known by anyone. As such, restrictions for shared accounts, outlined below, must be followed.

Shared Accounts: A shared account refers to an account for which several individuals either share the password or use the same authentication token. Shared accounts are only allowed when specific system or business constraints prevent the use of individual accounts. These occurrences need to be recorded by the information owner and reviewed by the Information Security Officer (ISO) or a designated security representative. Moreover, additional compensatory controls must be implemented to maintain accountability.

173

Shared accounts must

- Have the tokens (e.g., password) reset when any of its users no longer need access or otherwise in accordance with the Authentication Tokens Standard

- Be restricted to specific devices and hours when possible

- Wherever technically feasible, have its users log on to the system with their individual accounts and "switch user" (SU) or "run as" the shared account

- Have strictly limited permissions and access only to the system(s) required

Default Non-privileged Accounts: The default non-privileged account (guest or anonymous user) is an account for people who do not have individual accounts. This account type must

- Be inactive until required

- Have restricted rights and permissions

- Only be permitted following a risk assessment

- Have compensatory controls that entail limited network access

- Be allocated a password that users cannot alter but is changed monthly at a minimum by an administrator

- Not permit the account to be delegated to another account

- Maintain a log of users to whom the password is provided

Emergency Accounts: Emergency accounts are designed for short-term use, featuring limitations on their creation, origin, and usage, such as times and days allowed. SEs can create these accounts in reaction to emergencies, requiring quick activation. Consequently, the activation of emergency accounts may circumvent standard authorization procedures. Additionally, these accounts must be automatically deactivated after 24 hours.

Temporary Accounts: Temporary accounts are designed for brief use and come with restrictions on their creation, origin, usage (for instance, specific times or days) and must include designated start and stop dates. An organization may create temporary accounts during standard account activation processes to accommodate short-term account needs that do not require immediate activation, such as for vendors and manufacturers. These accounts must have strictly limited permissions and provide access solely to the necessary systems.

Version Control Table

Version Number	Purpose/Change	Author	Date

Policy Summary

These are what are the most important policies required for an SMB for securing your identity risks and Privileged Access Management. There are likely other policy documents that need to be documented and published. There are a number of resources for these if they don't already exist in your organization. For further reference, check out Chapter 6 and the section entitled "Resource Compendium."

Privileged Access Management Procedure

Given there aren't sufficient differences between SMB and the SME, we will cover this procedure in the Small and Medium Enterprises (SME) section below to keep this section as reasonably sized as possible. Scroll or flip through a few more pages to see this section covered.

Technology

Technology in this space can vary from the basics of a password manager to a larger enterprise-level solution perhaps managed by your Managed Service Provider or Cloud Service Provider. If your small business is truly a one-person operation, then a password manager (native in Apple's iOS or an add-on product you download) is likely sufficient. Be wary of where you download it and get it from a trusted source, like directly from the software maker's website or the Apple, Microsoft, or Android marketplaces.

Whenever possible, find an opportunity to move to passkeys on your devices and logins to lower the risk of exposure. Passkeys are a digital credential that often uses biometrics and allows a user to sign in to applications and websites without a password. A passkey is a digital credential tied to a specific device and user account, essentially a digital token that can be used to authenticate logins. The passkey relies on the user's device security (biometrics, PIN, or pattern) for authentication; when creating a passkey, a public/private key pair is generated and stored securely on the user's device. Users can log in without needing a username, password, or additional authentication factors.

As the data has shown, users typically are lazy with password choices, and this results in an easy break-in method by bad actors. In the technical weeds, passkeys combine private and public cryptographic keys to authenticate access by users, thus adding a level of security by avoiding passwords altogether.

Small and Medium Enterprises

This tier (SME) is often used more internationally and describes a set of companies and organizations that operate at a larger scale than SMBs but aren't a Large Enterprise size (over 1,000 employees and $1B in annual revenue). In this tier, SME, it is more often owned by a small group than an individual and can be incorporated or have other legal protections.

Small and Medium Enterprises will have between 101 to 500 employees, annual revenue of $10 million to $1 billion, and information technology specialists working internally. This ability to have internal technology specialists is one of the biggest differentiators (for the purpose of this book) between a SMB and SME organization. The leveraging of these resources allows the organization to have more ability to source and maintain these systems themselves. SMBs will have some capital expenditure (CAPEX) accounts that they will use to spend on technology and telecommunications.

Another differentiator in this tier is a SME company will have multiple locations to service and manage, adding complexity to the networking and security risks. Many of the companies in this tier are involved in manufacturing-type (noncommercial only) operations, though not exclusively. These companies being predominantly manufacturing is by-design as companies that "make things" require more than what a SME requires.

Small and Medium Enterprises are challenged to leverage the NIST Small Business guidance given they can often be just a bit oversized to leverage it. The advice here is to take a hybrid approach between the NIST Small Business guidance and NIST Cybersecurity Framework (NIST-CSF or equivalent framework) that the Large Enterprises (see below) will more often leverage. We will provide this guidance and documentation in the spaces below, but always be aware it may not be a "Cinderella" fit; meaning, the organization will likely have to adjust it to fit their specific use cases and situations. For example, while we focus on NIST-CSF and NIST Small Business, your team may leverage ISO 27001 or HITRUST. There are translators available (via a web search) that will provide a NIST-CSF to ISO 27001 that can help with this customization of fit.

People

Given that this type of business sits in that middle space between a Small and Medium Business and a Large Enterprise, they typically do not have enough staff to specialize in cyber and information technology personnel. In fact, given the complexities and pace of cybersecurity and technology risks, it is recommended that these organizations look to a Managed Service Provider (MSP) for assistance. The National Institute of Standards and Technology (NIST) has an excellent resource for SMB and SME organizations: "Choosing a Vendor/Service Provider."[8]

As the operator and/or owner of an SME, the need to procure and manage an MSP is a challenge in itself. Common questions:

- Do I need an MSP?

- How do I select the right MSP and support level?

- What types of MSPs are out there?

- What level of support is best for my organization?

- What contract terms are best for my SME and MSP?

- How best to manage the relationship with the MSP?

To determine if your organization requires a Managed Service Provider, the guidance is to answer some basic risk questions to determine the need to engage an MSP.[9] Use the list below to help determine your organization's risk and thus the need for assistance.

First, list all the data that your business or organization has that is sensitive or confidential. Determining if it is sensitive or confidential should be a question of: If this data or information about my customers or

---

[8] https://www.nist.gov/itl/smallbusinesscyber/guidance-topic/choosing-vendorservice-provider

[9] https://cyberreadinessinstitute.org/resource/should-i-get-outside-support-to-manage-my-cybersecurity-risk/

employees leaks out, would the regulators and/or the subjects of the data be able to sue me? Would this damage my business reputation enough to potentially make my organization file for bankruptcy or make business challenging to continue?

Second, list all the hardware and software (applications) that are crucial to running your business. This can be your website, email, data storage, financial systems, networking hardware, physical security hardware, and more. This may require you to reach out to others in the organization to determine the full scope of hardware and software that are needed to run the business.

Now take a risk-based approach to the lists created in steps one and two. Not all risks are equal, and thus, it is important to list the most critical to the least. It is tough to prescribe if the list should be only five or ten items long, and this is less important than the exercise of making it from highest risk to lowest risk. This is called a Business Impact Analysis (BIA). If there is some confusion over which is riskiest, take the approach of which items are required to operate the business day-to-day. What items from lists are required to "turn the lights on" and operate. Those are the riskiest. We can call those risks "Systemically Critical." The guidance from NIST calls them "your crown jewels." Again, the name is less important than the process of identifying what they are in risk-based order.

Once the team has identified the Systemically Critical items, the next step is to identify who has access to them. Some organizations are surprised by who they believe should have access to their data or devices compared to who actually has access when discovered or investigated. Also, take a look at whether it is protected or not.

Take the risk-based list of assets, and fill out the table below (if your organization has less than five or more than five, customize to your needs):

Risk Order	Data or Device	Description	Access	Protected	Regulatory
1	Customer database	50,000+ records of our customers with SSN and CC	Owner/CEO Sales rep Accounts receivable	Cloud Service Provider	Yes
2	Corporate website				
3	Corporate email				
4	Corporate accounting system				
5	Physical security system				

We've placed in the table some sample data to help with how your organization could populate it. In column 1, this is a simple risk-based listing that aligns to column 2 for whether it is a data or a device. Column 3 is to help describe the device or data to better detail what the risk presents to your business. The next two columns are designed to list who has access to them and if your organization believes they are adequately protected, or a more basic question of: Does anyone know if they are protected? The last column can be a simple yes or no but would benefit from a specific reference if there is a regulator who would be engaged if there is a breach or event for the data or device.

Review the results of the table, and if there is any doubt about columns four, five, and/or six (Access, Protected, Regulatory), then it is highly recommend that a Managed Service Provider should be engaged to lower the risk.

There are several different types of MSPs that can be leveraged, depending on the needs. An Information Technology (IT) or Cybersecurity Consultant is usually a small shop that has highly specialized persons or teams to assist with setting up hardware and/or software. These teams are great at specific projects or programs that have a fixed length, with a beginning and an end. This isn't to say they can't be leveraged for ongoing maintenance work, but they are not usually setup for this type of work.

Managed Service Providers are often SMEs on their own, with more than a dozen or more employees, where they engage in both project work and maintenance. An MSP is going to be geared to getting engaged with customers who are looking to outsource their IT needs to their teams. There is another type of MSP, called a Managed Security Services Provider (MSSP), where there is a team of credentialed and specialized cybersecurity teams. The MSSP will perform a host of cyber functions, such as penetration testing, intrusion detection and prevention, process and procedure development, and proactive cybersecurity responses. Lastly, there can be a Virtual Chief Information Officer (vCIO) or Virtual Chief Information Security Officer (vCISO) that can assist in providing much-needed leadership in these domains. It is kind of like renting an expert and can provide good help when sourced correctly.

Risk-Based List of Risks

Once your team has completed the list of data or technology that pose the greatest risk to your organization, ensure they are in priority (risk-based) order. Then, ask some basic questions about your comfort or ability to manage these risks:

- Does my company have to comply with any known regulations?

- Does my company have any sensitive data?

    - Such as Personally Identifiable Information (PII) which is two or more pieces of data that can identify an individual. Such as name and address or name and birthdate

    - Or Protected Health Information (PHI) which is data that contains health-related or medical information about your customers

- Do any of my customers (or my company) do business in states with privacy laws?

    - In particular, the California privacy law can likely ensnare a large percentage your customer base given the large population (and thus customers).

- Does my company accept credit card payments?

- Does my company fall within a "critical infrastructure"?

    - If you are unsure, check out this Cybersecurity and Infrastructure Security Agency (CISA) website on Critical Infrastructure Security and Resilience that takes time to provide examples: `https://www.cisa.gov/topics/critical-infrastructure-security-and-resilience/critical-infrastructure-sectors`.

If your answer to any of these questions is affirmative (and especially if you answer "yes" to more than one), then it is recommended your organization look into an MSP or MSSP to manage these important risks.

Process

In this tier, Small and Medium Enterprises, the teams can use the SMB process documents provided above with a few differences to account for the international or sector-specific regulatory and environmental risks. Rather than add a laundry list of potential international or sector-specific guidance here, we'll point the reader to look in the "Resource Compendium" section of Chapter 6 where we will provide links to resources relevant to this section and others. Start with the policy documents provided in the SMB, and add any localization or industry-specific regulatory requirements. Some of the businesses in this space can be in what are considered "highly regulated," and so, pay attention to that if your business is one of those. If you're unsure, seek some legal counsel or other expert in this field to help determine if you are overexposed to regulatory and compliance issues than other industries or enterprises.

Privileged Access Management Procedure

For organizations of this size, the documentation for the Privileged Access Management Procedure should be in simple business language and provide a checklist approach to lend themselves better to non-cyber, nontechnical staff to accomplish them when needed. A great resource for this is the National Institute of Standards and Technology (NIST) Cybersecurity Framework 2.0 Small Business Quick-Start Guide.[10] On the Protect page, there is guidance on what a small business should be prioritizing for access and Privileged Access Management. The following will be a template for readers in this space to use for their procedure. We encourage customization to account for your own organization's needs.

---

[10] https://nvlpubs.nist.gov/nistpubs/SpecialPublications/NIST. SP.1300.pdf

Privileged Access Management is critical to the success of our organization in protecting our customer data and resilience of operations. This will take six steps to complete and should be done on a regular basis by owners of systems that contain data or manage access to systems that are sensitive.

Define

A privileged account is defined as any account that has rights on a system or application that gives them the ability to make changes, special abilities, or special access beyond a normal user. This can be a person or a system account and usually is a trusted and authorized user who performs security-related functions that ordinary users cannot perform.

List accounts in your organization that fit the definition of "privileged":

Account	User	Complex Password Forced?	MFA Enabled?	Default Password Off?	Date Last Reviewed
Bank account					
Accounting/tax account					
Google, Microsoft, Apple ID, or similar					
Email account					
Password manager					
Website manager					
Social media manager					

Complete this table, customize it to your organization's needs, and set a regular schedule to complete it, update it, and make appropriate changes where needed.

Discover

Using the table above, the team will discover which systems and users have elevated privileges. This will be done on a regular basis of no less than twice in a calendar year. The owner of each system that has privileged access is required to complete this document and participate in the assessment when required.

Manage

The owners of each of these systems (bank account, email accounts, website manager, social media accounts, etc.) are responsible for managing the risk of privileged access of the systems. Proactively manage and monitor privileged account access with password protection software and password managers. Ensure that there is always the approach of least privilege, meaning that only those who have a business need for elevated access are given that level of access.

Monitor

Ensure that logging and auditing of the logs are done for systems where privileged access occurs. If this is automated with a security log aggregator like a Security Information and Event Manager (SIEM), that's better, but if that is not possible, the system owner is responsible to ensure there is a manual process that is reviewed for this access on a regular (at least monthly) reviews.

Respond

When an incident (or suspected incident) takes place, rely on the incident response plan, and focus on the steps around a privileged access account compromise incident. Changing the password or disabling the account will not be adequate to stop the damage of an incident, event, or breach. The response may require contacting an outside Managed Security Service Provider (MSSP) should the impact be beyond the capabilities of in-house staff.

Audit

Continuous monitoring of privileged account activity is a must and follows the Monitor stage above. Adopt an automated tool, if possible, to assist with ensuring the logs are readable and can be done a regular basis. If this is not done, a regular audit of privileged account activity, your organization will find out way too late that your data has been exfiltrated and are the subject of a phishing attack.

Technology

One of the best technology solutions in this business category is a password manager, and in fact, the National Institute of Standards and Technology (NIST) updated guidance in its Second Public Draft of Digital Identity Guidelines for Final Review[11] emphasizes the use of password managers as a great solution to lower the risk of password compromise for privileged accounts. Passwords should be long and random, with a recommendation for a minimum of 15 characters, while a shorter length is acceptable when paired with multifactor authentication. Leveraging password managers will assist with the adoption of these longer, complex, random passwords that are preferred and best practice.

---

[11] https://www.nist.gov/news-events/news/2024/08/nist-releases-second-public-draft-digital-identity-guidelines-final-review

As far as recommending password managers, at the time of this book being written, there are a number of solutions. Many are built within browsers or operating systems, and these small, point solutions will be fine for a one- or two-person small business; if there are more than a few people, the recommendation would be to look for a commercial, off-the-shelf (COTS) product that fits the needs of your organization. A simple web search will produce a variety of results and providing that list in this book will be dated within a few weeks of publication. However, PC Mag Online produced a great analysis of the current COTS products on the market in 2024.[12]

Lastly, we would recommend a tool to manage the logs and privileged account activity in your small enterprise. However, the better option is to look to an MSP or MSSP as described earlier to perform this function. If you are determined to perform this control monitoring on your own, then we would recommend a few searches for open source/free Security Information and Event Management software. At the time of this writing, there are a few we can recommend:

- Apache Metron

- The ELK Stack

- SIEMOnster

- Prelude

- OSSIM

---

[12] https://www.pcmag.com/lists/best-password-managers?cq_src=google_ads&cq_cmp=21236574468&cq_con=164144584720&cq_term=password+manager&cq_med=&cq_plac=&cq_net=g&cq_pos=&cq_plt=gp&gad_source=1&gbraid=0AAAAAD6oLYx52d-STqANIVugTd3-qGxgK&gclid=CjOKCQiAO--6BhCBARIs ADYqyL-ET3dLL-OdHc1dbio35Q5A9czezQYjlBqmtnfyULS25LqzbmfL_yYaAoTnEALw_wcB&test_uuid=O2O7EHHBhY2fKps8iRXlYNR&test_variant=C

These SIEM tools are "free" and so involve no licensing costs; however, one of the biggest "costs" of any of these types of monitoring software is the time and experience it takes to set it up and manage it. Whether your organization chooses to leverage one of the free tools and learn how to use it properly or your team engages a Managed Security Service Provider, it is very important to ensure you're watching what is going on in your enterprise. The best way to do that is with a SIEM and an active program to monitor and react.

Small and Medium Enterprises are a large portion of the overall businesses in operation and tend to be the larger commercial and small industrial businesses that are important to our economy. There are some differences with SMB in terms of complexity and breadth of coverage, as well as a higher likelihood that this business will be in a highly regulated environment. Be sure to pay attention to what regulatory bodies are overseeing your operations and could potentially make your business challenging. Also, document your policy and procedures leveraging what we've placed in this book. If it isn't written down, then it is being done differently each time and therefore ad hoc by nature. Regulators frown on this type of a program and expect to see something repeatable and scalable.

Large Enterprises

The Large Enterprise tier is the one most of us think of when faced with a multinational or national company. These have over 1,000 employees with an annual revenue over $1 billion. At this scale, there are full-time information technology and cybersecurity personnel at the organization. Indeed, there are specializations within these IT and cyber teams. In the previous tier, Small and Medium Enterprises, the IT team is much smaller (two to five personnel), and so, they wear "many hats" as they are responsible for more than one capability and/or service.

In the United States, according to the latest Small Business Administration data, there are just over 21,000 businesses that fit this category. While it is a small number, these companies employ a large number of people and have a large influence on the economies, both locally and nationally. These businesses often appeal to a large audience of customers across a very wide geographic map—at a national or international level. Large Enterprises have separate departments for functions: legal, IT, cybersecurity, marketing, sales, human resources, and so on. These departments have their own experts and management teams that require the IT and cyber teams to work directly with to ensure their needs are met.

The LE organizations have large headquarters and operations in their home country but often have operations and personnel in other countries around the world. These other teams can be sales, support, and even research and development. Very often, these overseas or offshore operations are monitored by the parent company from their primary location. As an example, it is common for a Large Enterprise US-based company to have call centers and Business Process Outsourcing (BPO) in India and/or the Philippines to provide support and development teams. The IT and cybersecurity teams will be headquartered in the US location but will be responsible for the overseas operations.

People

In this operation, there are a number of specialties in the enterprise involved in cybersecurity, Identity and Access Management (IAM), and Privileged Access Management (PAM). The complexity of the operations, their size, and coverage, along with the technologies and tools, mean that personnel in this space can become highly specialized and concentrated on a particular domain within cybersecurity. Let's take a look at some of the typical roles in PAM and IAM:

- IAM Systems Architect

- IAM Systems Engineer

- IAM Access Control Specialist

- IAM Administrator

- IAM Analyst

These roles can have slightly different names and levels across the spectrum. Definitions for what these roles do, how to best screen for candidates, and more are best formulated by your organization's needs and current available labor pool and the ability for those two to meet on an agreeable salary and employment terms. For best results, consult a good guide on the Identity Management Institute's website on Identity and Access Management Jobs.[13]

Process

The process in this operation, much like the people, is complex and has multiple lines of defense which means the documentation of process is also more involved than a SMB or SME operation. Much like those smaller organizations, there must be policies and procedures documented, published, reviewed, and communicated that are best practice.

Most organizations in this space will already have existing documentation or should have this already completed. However, it is not uncommon to find a Large Enterprise that has not documented this at all, has done insufficient documentation, or has not reviewed it in recent years, and it is now out-of-date. Rather than place templates for our readers to leverage, which will take up quite a lot amount of space in the book, we have found several locations where there are "free"

---

[13] https://identitymanagementinstitute.org/identity-and-access-management-jobs/

versions of these documents for download. Use them as you need them: compare your existing documentation for gaps, or use them to create documentation where none exists.

One of the largest areas where this documentation exists is at the SysAdmin, Audit, Network, and Security (SANS) Institute's website.[14] There are a number of policy documents here for use that would be great as a starter for most organizations of any larger size:

- Acceptable Use Policy

- Cyber Security Incident Recovery

- Database Credentials Policy

- Dial-in Access Policy

- Information Logging Standard

- Ethics Policy

- Password Protection Policy

- Remote Access Policy

- Server Security Policy

- VPN Policy

There are dozens of others on this site that can be leveraged for any Large Enterprise that needs policy documentation from scratch or a refresh of existing artifacts.

The Center for Internet Security has put together a number of policy documents from experts in the field and has templates on their website.[15] There is a workbook that can be downloaded and as of the writing of

---

[14] https://www.sans.org/information-security-policy/?per-page=100
[15] https://www.cisecurity.org/controls/policy-templates

this book is on version 8.1.[16] There are a number of policy templates for download:

- Acceptable Use Policy Template

- Account and Credential Management Policy Template

- Incident Response Policy Template

- Audit Log Management Policy Template

- Data Recovery Policy Template

- Audit Log Management Policy Template

- Vulnerability Management Policy Template

- Secure Configuration Management Policy Template

Lastly, the Commonwealth of Virginia's IT Agency has a listing of great IT security policy and procedures templates available on their website.[17] These examples are more "government" in their style, as compared to the "commercial" style in the other document sites listed above. The list on the Virginia site is quite extensive:

- Business Impact Analysis Policy Template

- Emergency Response Damage Assessment Procedure Template

---

[16] https://learn.cisecurity.org/cis-controls-download?_gl=1*1pmb
dyd*_gcl_aw*RONMLjE3MzQxOTM1ODAuQ2p3S0NBaUE5dlM2QmhBOUVppd0FKcG5Y
d3hkbHRJZnlUmNCcDhCUUw1bVR3YU1aWUdwanNtWndyNWpKcDFKRTJiRGN4R01BM
ENFZW5obONyVzhRQXZEXOJ3RQ..*_gcl_au*Mjg4MjE3NTA1LjE3MzQxOTM1NzE.
*_ga*MTEwNDY4NDY5Mi4xNzMOMTkzNTY4*_ga_N7OZ2MKMD7*MTczNDE5MzU2Ny4xLjEu
MTczNDE5MzY5MC4xOC4wLjA.*_ga_3FW1B1JC98*MTczNDE5MzU2Ny4xLjEuMTczNDE5M
zY5MC4wLjAuMA..

[17] https://www.vita.virginia.gov/policy--governance/policies-
standards--guidelines/it-security-policy--procedure-templates/

- Emergency Response Employee Communications Procedure Template

- Enterprise Background Check Policy Template

- Information Resource Acceptable Use Policy Template

- Information Security Incident Reporting Procedure Template

- Information Security Incident Response Procedure Template

- Information Security Program Policy Template

- Information Security Roles and Responsibilities Policy Template

- IT Configuration Management Policy Template

- IT Contingency Planning Policy Template

- Identification and Authentication Policy Template

- IT Incident Response Policy Template

- IT Media Protection Policy Template

- IT Personnel Security Policy Template

- IT Risk Assessment Policy Template

- IT Security Assessment and Authorization Policy Template

- IT Security Audit, Monitoring, and Logging Policy Template

- IT Security Exception and Exemptions Policy Template

- IT Systems and Communications Encryption Policy Template

- IT System and Communications Protection Policy Template

- IT System and Data Classification Policy Template

- IT System and Information Integrity Policy Template

- IT System and Services Acquisition Policy Template

- IT System Maintenance Policy Template

- IT System Security Planning Policy Template

- IT System Logical Access Controls Policy Template

- Mobile Device Access Controls Policy Template

- Physical Environmental Protection Policy Template

- Remote and Wireless Access Controls Policy Template

- Risk Treatment Plan Template

- Security Awareness and Training Policy Template

There are at least three sites we've found with excellent resources for creating or updating policy documentation for Large Enterprises. Ensure that your team is tailoring it to your organization's needs and not just taking it as-is. If it doesn't meet your actual process, then it is not going to be effective and will be a source of findings and issues. If you're starting from scratch (no policy documentation at all), then work with the other stakeholders for each policy to be sure the process and policy match what is actually happening in the enterprise. If you're looking to update or improve your documentation with the templates from the websites, in a similar vein, there will be a need to work with the business owners for each system to ensure the policy updates match what is actually occurring in your enterprise.

Regarding the procedures for Identity and Access Management and Privileged Access Management, there are also a number of resources available online. However, there are often too many variables in each organization to prescribe the process or procedure documentation. Instead, let's provide the reader with a process on creating this type of documentation, with a reminder about the PAM process as we described in Chapter 1.

In Chapter 1, we described the four steps for successful PAM life cycle and the Magnificent Seven PAM Best Practices. Privileged Access Management requires a life cycle to ensure these elevated accounts are governed and managed correctly and in a manner that minimizes the risk to the organization. The main purpose of this book is to demonstrate that this is not a "one and done" task: assign privileged access to the account, rotate it every 90 days, and consider "mission accomplished." That is called compliance and is not to be confused with cybersecurity. Cybersecurity requires ongoing due diligence and due care, and the same holds true for Privileged Access Management. It is a process that is continual and must be documented and mapped for users to better understand.

Many current life cycles have seven steps, and there is nothing wrong with these, but our approach is to bring it up a level to four main stages:

- Define and Discover
- Onboarding
- Monitor and Audit
- Offboarding

Each of these stages has a logical order and control flow. In Define and Discover, the effort is to define what PAM is at your organization and find out what meets that definition. This is a significant effort that then leads to a decision and action stage: Onboarding. This leads to the Monitor and Audit stage, where activities occur around those "onboarded" accounts that are put into a continuous monitoring effort. Lastly, as with everything, these accounts must eventually end, and there is a last decision and action stage: Offboarding.

Define and Discover

Define what "Privileged Access" means in your enterprise. We've provided one in this book from the National Institute of Standards and Technology, but that may not be clear enough or specific for your organization. Writing this down in a Privileged Access Management policy or standard is vital. Having this written down as a definition ensures everyone in your enterprise is working on the same definition and, therefore, with the same goal in mind.

In this case, Define also means all the other parts of PAM that go into the governance bucket. At the top level, an enterprise should have a cybersecurity policy or standard that mentions privileged access, defines it, and provides a reference to the appropriate PAM policy/standard document for more details. The Privileged Access Management policy/standard will contain definitions for important terminology, designate control points, and reference downstream documents such as runbooks and procedure documents.

Once a definition of Privileged Access is agreed upon, the discovery step involves both the accounts subject to the definition and their relative risk to the organization. This relative risk ranking allows for a risk-based approach to determining which accounts to take to the next stage of Onboarding first.

Onboarding

Onboarding resources into your PAM process requires planning with the end user in mind and your security outcomes. As users determine they will need an elevated account, requesting, approving, and retrieving privileged access tokens must be well mapped out, documented, and auditable. The onboarding process should include some control points to ensure elevated account approvals are appropriately approved and reviewed. Based upon both the role and risk, there need to be approvals for that privileged access. For example, if it is a new payroll clerk who needs access to the payroll system at a level to process paychecks, then that needs their manager approval. However, for the person or role who approves the whole company payroll to be sent for payment requires two approvals, both the CFO and the CEO.

Onboarding must take into account the items we discussed in lowering the risk to elevated accounts: just-in-time access, MFA, rotating passwords, etc. A workflow should be developed that is able to be followed by the end users who will be requesting a privileged account. This workflow should demonstrate the control or decision points, ensure it is clear what roles perform each step, and allow for a service turnaround time. Ideally, this onboarding will be automated to lessen the chances for transpositional error and speed up time to completion.

Monitor and Audit (Attestation)

Monitoring and Auditing is an ongoing monitoring process as to the five W's: who, what, where, when, and how elevated accounts are utilized. Much like the implementation step of Monitor and Audit, this step intends to have personnel and tools monitoring access rights. When a role meets the definition of privileged access, it is dealt with according to the governance model. The audit or attestation step is done regularly (with elevated accounts, it should be done at least quarterly for best practice) to review users' roles and access to determine if it is still required. This step lowers the risk of someone getting "privilege creep": users' jobs and roles change over time if that access is not reviewed and adjusted appropriately and their rights become elevated in a slow or "creep."

With the refresher on PAM life cycle completed, we can explain there are seven steps for a successful process documentation. Along the way, we will create a demonstration of the just-in-time access process documentation for readers to help. After we explain each of the process steps, there will be a short paragraph explaining how a just-in-time (JIT) access process documentation could be conducted.

Process Documentation Steps:

1. Define scope

2. Identify stakeholders

3. Collect information

4. Create visual

5. Test

6. Feedback

7. Publish

Define scope is the first and often the most important step as it ensures that goal is defined. Identify the specific process to be documented and published. Determine why the documentation is needed, for example, for compliance or ensuring training of new hires. Ensure that there is a start and end point for the process. If it is an end-to-end process, not tied to any other process, indicate that explicitly. If it is part of a longer process, indicate which process initiates the start and what process it ends with a handoff. Lastly, if needed, consider having a list of "Not in Scope" to declare what the process will not solve or tackle.

JIT scope is defined as limited to those whose permissions are defined as "privileged" by the enterprise. This scope is confined to logical access, not physical access.

Identify stakeholders is important to ensure that all involved or impact by the process are engaged. This list can include the teammates who perform the tasks, their managers, or external parties who interact with the process. List all the roles involved in the process, the subject matter experts (SMEs) who can be engaged, and identify who are the decision-makers among your stakeholders who can approve and provide feedback on the process documentation.

JIT stakeholders are identified as the business owners of the systems with sensitive data and critical infrastructure in the enterprise. Also, the leader of the PAM program and one of the analysts on their team is involved in documenting the process.

Step 3, collect information, involves interviewing and listening to the various folks involved in the system and process on the steps. Items to document are the duration of the process, time commitments for each employee, resources required to complete at each step, software or systems required, the methodology, and the chronological order in which they must be accomplished.

As the stakeholders meet and collect information about the JIT process at our organization, we document that the process has five steps: request for access, verification and approval, access granting, activity monitoring, and automatic revocation. The first three steps, from request for access to access granting, should take no longer than one minute, as determined by the stakeholders. The IAM team will perform much of the steps, with a need for the approval to be done by the requestor's manager.

The next step is to create a visual representation of the process as documented. The visual needs to use simple language and avoid acronyms. Provide enough information on the visual for viewers to understand the process from start to finish. Be short and concise, but provide enough information for readers to understand the concept.

Testing the workflow is the best way to validate that steps have been correctly documented and the logic works. This can be best done by doing something like a tabletop exercise with all the stakeholders to determine if it works. Identify any gaps and document them for adjustments if needed.

To test the process, the team would take a "fake" JIT ticket and walk it through the process to determine if it would be successful. In a real-world scenario, this would be an iterative process and allow for adjustments required for the process to go from start to finish.

Feedback from stakeholders is critical to gauge success. When meeting with stakeholders, always keep the scope handy in your discussion. It can be tempting for stakeholders or participants to get into scope creep and start adding things that this isn't designed to solve. Ask the stakeholders if the documentation is easy to understand, if it is accurate, and if it would be helpful to other teammates. Determine if there is too much or too little information provided.

Publish the process. If it isn't available to those internal to your organization, then it isn't a process. This can be done on an intranet or a tool designed for pushing out policy and process documentation. It must have a version control and must be revisited and reviewed at least annually.

At our demo organization, once the team documented the process, created the visual, gotten feedback from stakeholders, made the necessary adjustments to get it right, they went and published the process on the internal company intranet and made an announcement over company-wide distribution list. It explained where to find the document, what were its effective dates, who approved it, and what is covers.

Technology

The technology for Privileged Access Management at Large Enterprises is a big business for many solution providers. There are a few very large software solution makers in this space, and we will discuss a few of them, to provide examples of the solutions. The authors make no endorsement of any particular solution but want to provide insight into what types of capabilities users would typically look for when looking for a PAM software solution.

Visibility and Threat Intelligence

Most organizations lack a centralized view of identities and their privileged access account usage. The tool solution should have a holistic view of all the identities in your enterprise, whether on-premises or in the cloud. The benefit of being able to get visibility onto the attack paths from identity risks is key. This will enable your team to have actionable intelligence and get threat investigations done quicker and more completely.

Implement Least Privilege

Privilege creep is what this is primarily designed to thwart. It is far too common in enterprises to see users with over-inheritance or overprivileged accounts due to a variety of factors. The technology your team chooses must be able to identify local administrative users across all your operating systems. It should audit and inform when this rule has been violated (there should not be local administrators for good hygiene). The ability to get granular control on your deployed applications is crucial for least privilege to be successful.

Secure Remote Access for All

Hybrid and remote work are here to stay; add to this all the third parties and partners organizations work with and nearly 100% of a company is remote at some point and will need access. The solution must allow for granular access to specific applications or systems, not an all-or-nothing approach. The remote access control should also allow for geo-fencing and time controls as well.

Improve Accountability and Control

"You can't control what you don't measure" is still a true statement. Without a way to have accountability and control into your list of privileged accounts, then there will be no way to spot trouble or manage the large list of users. The technology solution must have a way to automatically discover privileged or elevated accounts and credentials in the environment. And it must be for both human and machine-based accounts. The solution would be ideal if it automatically identified these accounts and magically moved them into a privileged management process for better control.

Streamline Identity Management

Lastly, with all the other capabilities in a PAM solution, there is no requirement to have a single solution for identity management to achieve the best outcome. While it can be considered "better" to have a single solution, it is often difficult to achieve and may not be the ideal outcome. The centralization of the login and configuration management for Unix, Linux, and Windows-based systems ensures nothing gets missed anymore, but this may require correlating more than two systems. Whether it is three systems or more or a single solution, there is a requirement to have a streamlined, (near)-automated process to have it repeatable and scalable. This is the automation that modern PAM systems require.

Chapter Summary

In this chapter, we discussed the case studies, along with how to implement PAM successfully with a focus on the policy and program documentation. Because many organizations include Privileged Access Management inside their Identity and Access Management process and program documentation, there is an inclusion of this larger context (IAM, not just PAM alone) to provide a complete picture for readers:

- Case Studies: Overview of what is involved in making a product PAM environment ready

- Small and Medium Businesses: Provide detailed example of successful PAM implementations in the smallest organizations

- Small and Medium Enterprises: Provide detailed example of different PAM implementations in these medium-sized companies

- Large Enterprises: Provide how the largest organizations can accomplish PAM implementations

CHAPTER 5

Blueprint for Successful Implementation

Chapter Overview

- Project Management Methodologies: Incorporate project management methodologies specific to cybersecurity implementations.

- Stakeholder Management: Discuss strategies for managing various stakeholders during implementation.

- Sustainability and Scalability: Focus on how to maintain and scale PAM solutions over time.

- Plan of Action:

  - Planning

  - Execution

  - Governance

© Gregory C. Rasner, Maria C. Rasner 2025
G. C. Rasner and M. C. Rasner, *Privileged Access Management*,
https://doi.org/10.1007/979-8-8688-1431-0_5

- Root cause analysis

- Operationalize

- Metrics for success

- PAM in DevOps: Discuss the role of PAM in DevOps environments.

- Cloud vs. Non-cloud: Discuss how PAM/ZT differs based on an organization's use of cloud or non-cloud technologies and how they can adapt to their infrastructure realities.

- Human vs. Machine Access: Break down how PAM/ZT needs to work for human-to-machine access vs. machine-to-machine access. Tie back to identity management (person vs. machine identity).

- Tools and Technologies

- PAM for IoT: Explore the challenges and solutions for managing privileged access in IoT and other emerging tech.

- Sector-Specific Challenges: Address sector-specific challenges and solutions in PAM implementation.

- Third-Party Access

- Best Practices and Pitfalls: Share best practices and common pitfalls across different scenarios.

Project Management and Implementation

Implementing Privileged Access Management requires it be a project. A project is defined as something that has a start and an end date, as opposed to a maintenance activity which is ongoing and has no foreseen end date. A project management plan for Privileged Access Management (PAM) implementation should focus on identifying all privileged accounts within an organization, classifying their access levels, implementing strong authentication methods, monitoring privileged sessions, and continuously reviewing access rights all while adhering to the principle of least privilege to minimize security risks; key steps include discovery, classification, policy definition, solution selection, deployment, user training, and ongoing monitoring with clear project phases, deliverables, timelines, and responsible parties assigned to each stage. There are four project stages: Initiation, Planning, Execution, and Closure.

The Initiation phase is the first step in starting a project, and this is where the team will be determining the value of the project, who are the key stakeholders, and the scope. Define the project scope to determine where are the critical systems, sensitive data, and the target privileged user roles that will require Privileged Access Management. Establish the project goals and objectives that clearly describe the security improvements and compliance obligations where appropriate. Determine who are they key stakeholders as they will be key decision-makers and are likely the business leaders for each impacted organization. Form the project team around that key stakeholders by determining key architecture, engineering, and business staff. Develop and publish a project charter that documents the project scope, overall goals, schedule, resources, and budget. Clearly define what "success" looks like, and ensure it is measurable.

The Planning phase is built off the work done in Initiation. Perform account discovery to get a thorough inventory of all privileged accounts across the enterprise, including service accounts and local administrators. Classify the privileged accounts into categories based upon the risk they present to your organization (high, medium, low) so the team can take a risk-based approach as the project develops. A risk assessment for each of the areas will identify potential threats for the privileged accounts and help with the prioritization of the solutions. Develop policies based upon this prioritization and clearly defined access control policies based upon least privilege, MFA, session logging, and strong authentication methodology.

The Execution phase takes the hard work done in the first two phases, and it is where changes start to take place in Production. Install and configure the chosen PAM implementation (see below section) across the defined systems for the project. Testing and validation will need to be done on a non-production system and then to the production system to ensure all issues are resolved before onboarding begins. Users can be onboarded using a training process for the updated password management, access requests, and session management changes. There will need to be a period of "Access Remediation" as there often needs to be adjustments to user accounts and policies to get the best practice outcome.

The Closure phase involves closing-out the project to ensure all the deliverables, within the defined scope, are completed and the key stakeholders have signed off on it. Once all the deliverables have been agreed as completed, there should be a post-implementation evaluation to analyze the effectiveness of both the project team and the project outcomes. In addition, one of the most important checklist items on this phase is the "turning over" operation from the project team to the IAM and/or PAM team that will manage this day-to-day.

PAM Implementations

There are a number of use cases for implementing Privileged Access Management, and the National Institute of Standards and Technology (NIST) provides some great guidance on how these can be implemented for the enterprise in NIST-SP1800.[1] This document provides some examples of how the authors used COTS and open source tools to accomplish PAM in these implementations.

---

[1] https://www.nccoe.nist.gov/sites/default/files/legacy-files/fs-pam-nist-sp1800-18-draft.pdf

PAM in Infrastructure

In this implementation, the intent is to illustrate how networking devices, servers, databases, applications, desktops, etc., are designed to use PAM optimally. The normal users here would be administrators configuring hardware, performing updates on server operating systems, or pushing out updates to desktops. Users in this space are typically system or network administrators.

While the NIST illustration provides specific products to be used, we will anonymize the product names in order to not appear to be endorsing a particular product—and because it is more about the process than the specific solution selected:

- PAM Server

- Monitoring Agent

- Active Directory

- SIEM tool

- ITSM (IT Service Management)

- Authenticator tool

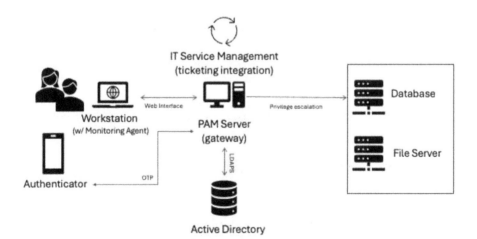

Figure 5-1. *Infra PAM Implementation*

In this implementation, there is a monitor on the privileged user's activity on their desktop workstation. The administrator should perform these duties from a dedicated administrator workstation, desktop, or laptop. There is a server that provides the privileged user access control interface where the escalation will occur once approved. The PAM Server requests the user is authenticated from their account information and is authenticated by the user store in the active directory. There is an Authenticator tool used to provide a second-factor of authentication (MFA) and further assure that the user is who they say they are.

At the top of the figure, there is a "IT Service Management" (ticketing integration) icon that is representative of the opportunity to integrate this into a ticketing system. This is a crucial automation step to ensure the timely capture and resolution of PAM requests.

When the user is authenticated with username, password, and the OTP on the Authenticator tool, then the PAM Server provides a just-in-time (JIT) token to escalate the user on the target system. The user connects directly to the target system, and when their actions are done, the connection is terminated, and the user's permissions are lowered back to a normal user permissions (non-escalated). The process is as follows:

1. User connects to the PAM Server on a web interface and enters their username, password, and OTP from the Authenticator tool.

2. The PAM Server authenticates the user with the Active Directory.

3. The Active Directory returns the authentication response.

4. When the user is authenticated, the PAM Server validates the OTP.

5. The PAM Server checks that the user is permitted to have the escalated privileges on the target system.

6. The administrator logs directly into the target system user their username and password.

7. When the time runs out or the user manually disconnects, then the access is terminated.

This process is most often used for an elevated account to get access to a protected system, but the preference is to leverage just-in-time access to arrive at Zero Standing Privilege (ZSP) as a solution. This is where a normal user account gets the elevated access that is time-bound to perform the actions required. This ZSP solution is fully tractable and auditable and is the direction a lot of the leaders in this space are currently heading.

This implementation is a very typical use case for most enterprises as all of them will require administrator roles to perform project implementations, ongoing maintenance work, and emergency repair work. These roles require escalation, and the tools and process describe how to implement this solution for each of the instances where a sensitive system requires access.

PAM for Security Information and Event Management

The Security Information and Event Management tool is one of the most important security tools in the enterprise. SIEMs typically runs and is accessed via a management network, and they typically are only accessed by privileged users. There is a need to ensure PAM is implemented for any access and management of the SIEM tool.

In this use case, there a few more parts, but they are again anonymized for specific solutions:

- PAM Monitoring System
- PAM Server

- Authentication Server

- Privileged User Identity Store

- Active Directory

- SIEM

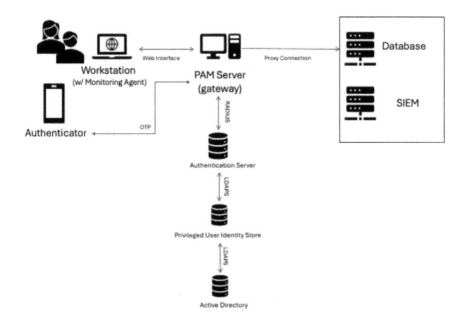

Figure 5-2. *PAM for SIEM*

The monitor agent is viewing and monitoring the activity on the administrator's desktop, and the desktop is dedicated to only performing these escalated functions. The PAM Monitoring System provides the PAM user control interface. The user is authenticated on the flow from the Authentication Server, to the Privileged User Identity Store, and then an authentication request to the Active Directory. The Authentication Server provides a OTP second factor of authentication for the privileged users.

PAM in Security Monitoring

Security monitoring, much like the SIEM, is a critical aspect of the security for the enterprise. Ensuring that there is a Privileged Access Management system to control access is equally critical. If you've implemented network segmentation for a Zero Trust network, then this becomes even more important to the success of your Zero Trust strategy. The critical parts in this implementation:

- Privileged Access Monitoring Workstation

- SIEM

- PAM

- Active Directory

- Production Enterprise

- MFA

- Privileged User Identity Store

There are many typical users in this space, from the cloud, directory, or system administrator. The NIST SP 1800-18B provides some use cases for when the security monitoring would involve a PAM solution.

Security Analyst: A security analyst in the enterprise need to access the system logs to investigate a server outage. In this scenario, there has been an alert or incident, and the analyst is going to access the logs for the incident. An analyst would open the SIEM and review the data, identify the affected items, and then gain access and review the logs for each of those items. Rather than performing the investigation this way, which does not provide enough details, leveraging a PAM system will ensure all privileged account activity is logged and each session is recorded. This data would be relayed to the SIEM and allow for better correlation of the data than having to dig into each item separately.

Business-Critical/High-Value Application Access: There are countless of these types of applications in our organizations nowadays. From a social media account to the HR system, from accounts payable to the customer database, there are tons of applications in our enterprise that are business-critical or high-value or both. In many environments, the accounts for social media accounts are often shared across teammates, in the very simplest of ways where the marketing teams will share the single username and password. With PAM system correctly deployed, these connections are logged and managed which would result in less likely insider threats and far less risk for breaches. Investigations in the event of a breach or incident are also easier due to the PAM solution deployment.

PAM for Application Layer

The overwhelming majority of our interactions are with applications and software in the enterprise. There are a number of examples on these types of accounts: access administrators, accounts payable administrators, human resources leadership, personnel managers, network administrators, marketing leaders, and many others we've not listed due to time and space constraints. The one common characteristic is these are accounts and users who have elevated access and permission within an application. Keep in mind the best practice is to have a dedicated PAM workstation for these users and not the same desktop that they do their day-to-day operations (web browsing, word documents, etc.). There are a couple parts in this use case:

- PAM Server

- Monitoring Agent

- RSA Authentication Manager

- Active Directory

- Privileged User Identity Store

- SIEM

214

The process for this implementation works in this order:

1. The privileged user connects to the PAM Server and provides their username, password, and a OTP from the RSA token (one could also use any other Authenticator application).

2. The PAM Server uses the Active Directory to validate the username and password, and the AD provides the response for authentication.

3. The PAM Server sends the RSA token to the RSA Authentication Manager using RADIUS or a Microsoft token to the Active Directory and the Privileged User Identity Store via Security Assertion Markup Language (SAML).

4. The RSA Authentication Manager or Active Directory validates the token and returns the approve or deny response to the PAM Server.

5. The PAM Server provides access to the application via direct access or a remote desktop application.

PAM in Development

We will cover the five main methodologies for software development: Agile, Waterfall, Rapid, DevSecOps, and DevOps. How you integrate PAM into these methods can vary slightly, but the principles are similar across the methods. The main differences can come in how and frequency of deployment in terms of people, process, and technology.

Agile Development

Agile development methodology is focused on iterations that contain micro-updates to new functionality and/or fixes. There are a number of types of Agile, such as scrum, extreme programming (XP), feature-driven development (FDD), and crystal. An advantage of Agile methodology is it allows for rapid deployment due to the use of iterations for releases; thus, software benefits happen earlier due to more frequent updates. However, this relies on a large commitment from the users in terms of communication to the development team and can be challenging on documentation updates to the frequent updates. In this methodology, it is best to have the PAM team or a representative on the project team because the sprints in this methodology mean there is a lot of back and forth. This is best handled if the key players are directly engaged with project team and PAM team. If this isn't possible due to resource or time constraints, then providing updates to the PAM team on changing elevated access requirements is crucial.

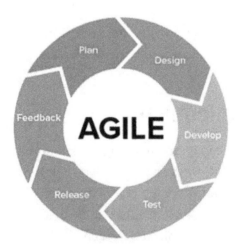

Figure 5-3. *Agile Methodology*

Waterfall Development

This is the traditional, old-school method of project management or development. The biggest advantage of this method is it is the easiest to adopt and learn since most folks are accustomed or familiar with this methodology. Waterfall methodology tends to be slower in pace than an Agile style just due to the difference in sprints vs. the "stages" that Waterfall lays out.

Where and how to engage the PAM and IAM resources in these projects can vary, but the best options are to have them engaged on the Initiation phase for scope discussions initially. If the product or service is identified as high risk or part of your Zero Trust Protect Surface, then having a IAM or PAM resource assigned to the project team is a requirement.

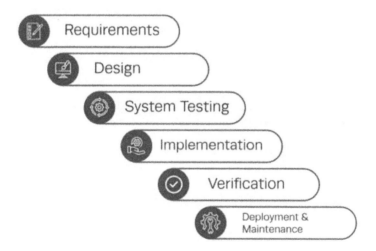

Figure 5-4. *Waterfall Methodology*

DevOps

Privileged Access Management in DevOps is crucial, given the reliance on software and the amount of software vulnerabilities. We should first define DevOps, a combination of "development" and "operations" that defines a set of tools, people, and processes to deliver applications and services faster and more efficiently than traditional methods. In the conventional model, the developers built the system or software, and the operations team tested and then provided feedback. This sent the development team off to fix the bugs and provide the updated code or system to the operations team so they could start the cycle over again.

In a DevOps model, the goal is to break down these typical barriers and have the people, process, and technology collaborate across the operations, development, quality assurance, and security teams. There are some common DevOps security gaps such as unsecure code, hard-coded passwords, vulnerable scripts, vulnerable CI/CD tools, over-provisioning privileges, secrets sharing, and misconfigurations of containers. Any PAM solution deployed into this development methodology should perform these control functions:

- Manage and audit all privileged sessions with visibility.

- Applies application level control to ensure least privilege access and use.

- Enforces least privilege.

- Discovers and manages all hard-coded passwords, keys, secrets, certificates, etc., including access to source code.

- Manages the boundaries between the environments (Dev, Test, Production) and deployment changes.

- Inventories and onboards all DevOps assets and workflows.

In DevOps space, another important security control is managing secrets (keys, certificates, etc...) to be managed properly. Inside the code, there are a lot of these secrets in the applications, and they must be protected. The best practice is to have an embedded IAM and/or PAM specialist in the DevOps team so security is built into the project.

PAM in Cloud

While the principles of Privileged Access Management don't change between the cloud and non-cloud (on-premises), however, how they can and are implemented is often different due to their respective challenges. Depending on how your organization decides to implement PAM: a single PAM solution that consolidates the privileged accounts (regardless of location) or if your organization will manage them in the cloud-native application. We will assume your organization is using the cloud-native solution and what is entailed in performing Privileged Access Management in the cloud environment.

All the major Cloud Service Providers have their PAM solutions. Google Cloud Platform (GCP) provides an overview on its PAM solution and describe how it provides just-in-time access for individuals along with audit logs.[2] Amazon Web Services provides some guidance on how to implement PAM solution on their platform leveraging the IAM Identity Center.[3] They use the acronym TEAM for Temporary Elevated Access Management solution that integrates with the AWS IAM Identity Center (which was AWS Single Sign-On). Microsoft created a new term "Privileged Identity Management" (PIM—which we discuss a bit below). The Azure product is called Entra, and it provides the just-in-time access with logging that one would expect for a PAM solution in the cloud.

---

[2] https://cloud.google.com/iam/docs/pam-overview
[3] https://aws.amazon.com/blogs/security/temporary-elevated-access-management-with-iam-identity-center/

Connectors are available for those who use an on-premises solution, and if your organization leverages one, then they are likely supported by one of the major Cloud Service Providers.

There are some advantages and disadvantages to an on-premises vs. a cloud-based PAM solution.

On-Prem:

- Direct Control: This is nothing new, but having the system on your network and under your control provides a level of assurance not provided in the cloud solution.

- (Potentially) Better Performance and Security: We use the term "potentially" because this depends on how your on-premises solution is resourced. However, if the system is correctly designed and operated, then having the PAM solution on-premises allows for improved performance.

- Large Upfront Cost: Some of these solutions can have a large upfront cost just to get the software installed and running. Then, you add in the annual maintenance, along with capacity management, and regular upgrades and deployments—now you're talking about real money that can be tough to justify in a tight budgetary environment.

- Discovery Challenges: These on-premises systems can be challenged to discovering the full breadth of privileged accounts and identities across a larger enterprise with lots of complexity.

Cloud:

- Easy to Deploy and Scale: One of the chief selling points of cloud in the first place is the ease to deploy and to scale up when needed. Or scale down when discovered you're overbuilt.

- Lower Upfront and Maintenance Costs: The large upfront costs for most software is spread out like a long-term rental in a SaaS solution for PAM. Capacity management and maintenance are nearly gone as a cost.

- Integration with Other Clouds: All of the Cloud Service Providers and PAM solution makers want you to use their site and product as their single pane-of-glass, and so, they have connectors for their PAM to integrate with their product as your single pane-of-glass for all clouds and on-prem.

- Locked into CSP, Limit on Customizations and Control: The downside is not too dissimilar from the on-premises solution but more pronounced when all your data belongs to a CSP provider for PAM.

Authors' Aside: PAM vs. PIM

Privileged Identity Management (PIM) is also a term used in this space, but it is not the same as Privileged Access Management (PAM). There are some subtle but significant differences. PIM provides time-bound, approval-required role activation and enforces temporary elevated (also referred to as just-in-time access) and least-privileged access to lower the risk of unnecessary and uncalled-for access to protected resources. PIM also encompasses policy controls to lower the risk, such as multifactor authentication (MFA) and temporary elevated access.

Privileged Access Management utilizes tools and technology to control and monitor how resources are accessed in your enterprise, leveraging concepts such as least privilege and time-bound access. Primarily, the PIM term is used around Microsoft and their Azure solution, but it can be found in other locations.

Human vs. Machine Access

Similar to the section above, the principles of PAM do not change between human vs. machine access. Machine accounts still need to be least privilege and part of your PAM program. However, due to the nature of the type of user (human vs. machine), how they are managed and secure can be different.

Service Accounts

Service accounts are found in all operating systems (Linux, Unix, Windows) and Cloud Service Providers. They are there to manage tasks, applications, operate virtual machines (VMs), automated services, batch scripts, and other automated, nonhuman accounts. The service accounts should have their dependencies mapped and centrally managed. Service account dependencies are accounts that represent resources, such as a Windows Service or Scheduled Tasks, that are accessed from a target machine and are also known as usages or dependent accounts.

Service accounts are often accounts that are shared across multiple assets to operate as a single resource. These accounts usually do not allow for a local login but can be misused or exploited due to their elevated privileges. Additionally, these accounts often fail to get recognized due to the way they are created, activated, and managed (or not).

Getting service accounts into your PAM solution is critically important, and they must be synchronized—or there is a risk that automated processes or services will not be performed as expected. Now you have to deal with an outage. As you perform your discovery across the enterprise for privileged accounts, be sure to include any instance where a service account might be used.

Robotic Process Automation (RPA) Accounts

These accounts emulate humans and are leveraged to build, deploy, and manage software bots to carry out automated tasks. The RPA accounts are privileged and very often share credentials to extract data and interact with the Cloud Service Providers and Application Program Interface (API). These accounts must never be shared but unique for each instance or service. These accounts would typically be used by a variety of administrators (network, security, system, application) and must be placed into your PAM system. Ensure there is a one-to-one relationship in the PAM solution for better management and visibility.

Cloud Accounts

These can be thought of as service accounts that are specialized in the cloud environment of a Cloud Service Provider (CSP). These accounts are used to manage cloud instances, workloads, runtime jobs, and resources. These accounts are usually managed within the CSP console and are based upon the identity, their entitlements, and their permissions. When performing discovery for these accounts, ensure there is an effort to explore the multicloud environments most organizations utilize to ensure full visibility.

Accounts with Embedded Credentials

While not preferred, there are dozens of reasons why credentials would be embedded in a script, configuration files, code, or automated tasks. It is definitely not best practice but it happens. These instances need to be discovered and catalogued for visibility and management. Ensure these credentials are placed in your PAM solution for proper management. A best practice would be that, once discovered, instances of embedded credentials are migrated into a normal process of credentials being provided outside the tool or service.

Access Reviews

There are owners for each of the systems using a machine account. If there is not an owner identified, then that is a critical step to complete as these machine accounts must go through the normal access review process as human accounts are required to complete. Access reviews are a critical step in auditing and monitoring privileged access accounts, and machine accounts must be part of that process, or it is only a matter of time before one or more of these accounts will be leveraged by a bad actor.

Tool and Technology Selection

In the following sections, we discuss a number of topics around tools and technology to assist the reader with selection and determining the best fit. As a reminder, the tools and technology are not the PAM solution but are part of the solution. Much like a general contractor who is going to build a home, having a machine saw and drill are important tools, but they are not the only tools needed to build the home. In fact, the general contractor will first start with plans of what the house is going to look like when completed along with building plans. The tools and technologies to build a house are a part of the whole set of planning, testing, designing, implementing, and other actions to get one built.

Checklist of Capabilities

As your organization looks to select (or reselect) a Privileged Access Management solution, there are some capabilities that a buyer should be aware of during the selection process. They can be broken down into a few groupings:

- Automation

  - Full network and cloud discovery with automatic onboarding of privileged accounts and identities

  - Full discovery of all secrets and keys

  - Automatic management of credentials across all platforms (Windows, Unix, Linux, cloud)

  - Automatic rotation of passwords, keys, and all other secrets on a defined schedule

  - Allows for connections to other security platforms (SIEM, ITSM, or SCIM, for example) to automate alerts across the enterprise

  - Allows for automation of workflows within the tool and externally to lessen chances for human error

  - A single pane-of-glass to manage both human and system privileged accounts

  - Automates application control to allow for better, granular control for elevated access to applications

  - Integrated with industry standards and platforms, from SAML and RADIUS to Kerberos

- Audit

  - Shows where and how privileged accounts are being used

  - Enforces session monitoring and management for a quality audit trail

  - Offers a REST API available for connectors.

  - Integrates all policies, roles and log data via https

- Alerts

  - Provides a way to alert to anomalous or risky behavior around privileged access and identities within the product or directly into the alerting tool of your organization's choice

  - Integrates across platforms for identity security, SIEM, ITSM, CMDB, and other critical monitoring and management software

  - Provides visibility into your third-party elevated access

  - Identifies potential vulnerabilities and misconfigurations to ensure they can be mitigated quickly

- Enforcement

  - Enforces least privilege

  - Enforces the Privileged Access Management policies, from password complexity, rotation, encryption, expiration, and other controls

  - Ensures no default or shared passwords are used

- Enforces session monitoring and management ensuring a good audit trail

- Enforces no local administrators as a rule

- Enforces policy-based restrictions on software installation and use

This list of capabilities is not exhaustive, and it will likely vary depending on the complexity of your enterprise. Always keep in mind that the technology and tools are not the outcome but things your team will use to get to the outcome. Also, be sure to ask about a Customer Success Team for each potential PAM solution provider—these are fairly common in many of the more complex, expensive solutions. Solution makers realize that it is a challenge to get this right, and having a Customer Success Team or point person will go a long way to your adoption of the technology.

Focus on Strategy, Not Cool

As you engage with PAM solution providers, there will be a lot of cool demonstrations provided. There will no doubt be some great solutions and technologies shared and demonstrated. It can be tempting to find a "solution" based upon these demonstrations without focusing on your strategy.

Strategy is the goal the organization is marching toward. Recall that in our earlier discussion of strategy, it can be challenging for our organizations in cybersecurity to focus on it. We tend to be focused on tactical issues, solving immediate problems without a thought to the long-term goals of the organization.

Always take your strategy with you into these demonstrations. If you don't take it physically, take it with you in your thoughts and how your team evaluates the tools and technology. Recommendations would be to have a predetermined set of questions for the vendors of these tools so there is a consistent evaluation. Identify those capabilities that are most critical (must-haves) vs. those that your team views as good-to-have or nice-to-have.

Stakeholder Management

Managing expectations is the key to success in most projects. Privileged Access Management project stakeholder management is the process of organizing communications and managing expectations with stakeholders in the project. A stakeholder is a person or group that has an interest in a project, is involved in its work, or could gain or lose something as a result of the project. Stakeholders can be internal or external to the organization and can be direct or indirect.

There are some basic recommendations for managing this important group during the project phase. First, identify the stakeholders. Understand their role, expectations, and their influence in the organization. Categorize the sponsors into internal or external, direct or indirect, and as positive or negative influencers. Create a stakeholder management plan that includes a list of these sponsors, a mapping of their hierarchical and organizational location, a prioritization listing of their criticality to the project success, and preferred communication format and style.

Regular engagement and involvement of the stakeholders is key to the success of this project. Attempt to understand the stakeholders' perspectives and what motivates them. Find out what is the benefit of the PAM solution to their area (more stable, more secure, compliance, etc.) to get better buy-in on decisions. Schedule regular meetings for updates to this group as well as to assist with any blockers or issues preventing progress. Always remember what the original scope of the project was to ensure there is no scope creep, and if needed, validate this with the stakeholders.

Example Plan of Action

In order to help illustrate how to implement a PAM solution project, we will take an example project. The example we will use here is an organization chooses the scope of third parties with privileged access to get into the PAM program and governance. We will make some of the example a bit simple to allow for brevity, and as you look to leverage, it can add the complexity in your real-world organization.

To make it more complete, here are some specifics for the sample run:

Our company is Widget Conglomerates (WC), and we make widgets and e-widgets. It is located in the United States and sells only within the United States. The company relies on three vendors for critical operations: Acme HR, Sales-R-Us, and FinanceSW. Acme HR is an online SaaS provider for all their human resources and payments. Sales-R-Us is an offshore Business Process Outsourcing (BPO) company that provides sales calls and customer support calls from the Philippines. FinanceSW is the online SaaS provider that does all the finance work required at Widget Conglomerates. There are 5,000 employees, and half are in the corporate headquarters (in Raleigh, North Carolina), and the rest are spread out throughout the United States.

The leader for the Identity and Access Management (IAM) team is Kristina, and she has been tasked by the Chief Information Security Officer (CISO) to start to initiate a PAM program and solution at Widget Conglomerates. She decides to start with what the senior leadership views as the riskiest privileged users: their third parties.

Initiation

Refresher: The Initiation phase is the first step in starting a project, and this is where the team will be determining the value of the project, who are the key stakeholders, and the scope. Define the project scope to determine where are the critical systems, sensitive data, and the target privileged user roles that will require Privileged Access Management. Establish the project goals and objectives that clearly describe the security improvements and compliance obligations where appropriate. Determine who are the key stakeholders as they will be key decision-makers and are likely the business leaders for each impacted organization. Form the project team around those key stakeholders by determining key architecture, engineering, and business staff. Develop and publish a project charter that documents the project scope, overall goals, schedule, resources, and budget. Clearly define what "success" looks like and ensure it is measurable.

The Initiation phase is kicked off by Kristina by identifying who are the key stakeholders. She identifies the business owners for each of the three vendors and also the engineers who manage the access management and the security monitoring tools required for PAM. Most importantly, Kristina gets a project manager assigned, Christian, to lead the project and guide it to success. Kristina manages a whole team of IAM professionals, and while she is capable of managing a project too, it is not best practice.

Christian, as the project manager, sets up a project scope definition discussion with the stakeholders. The project team is formed around the key stakeholders identified by Kristina—the business owners for the vendor relationships and the engineers who will manage the process—and holds a meeting to confirm details such as scope, resources, schedule, and budget. These four variables are documented to allow the project team to come back and judge their progress against these items. Christian also schedules a kickoff meeting and a regular meeting for stakeholders every two weeks and a project team meeting weekly.

Planning

Refresher: The Planning phase is built off the work done in Initiation. Perform account discovery to get a thorough inventory of all privileged accounts across the enterprise, including service accounts and local administrators. Classify the privileged accounts into categories based upon the risk they present to your organization (high, medium, low) so the team can take a risk-based approach as the project develops. A risk assessment for each of the areas will identify potential threats for the privileged accounts and help with the prioritization of the solutions. Develop policies based upon this prioritization and clearly defined access control policies based upon least privilege, MFA, session logging, and strong authentication methodology.

Once they've completed the steps above, the project manager Christian kicks off the Planning phase by initiating an inventory of all privileged accounts across the three vendors, including service accounts and local administrators. They classified the accounts into different risk categories of high, medium, and low. High were those privileged accounts that could bring an entire system offline or exfiltrate sensitive data. These high-risk categories also included those accounts that have ability to create application logins for other privileged accounts. Medium was defined as those accounts with elevated access but can only affect those accounts directly tied to that login. This risk category also included those accounts that can make single user and normal user accounts within the software or vendor environment.

Once they've got the list of privileged accounts in risk-based order, the team performs a risk assessment of each of the three vendor environments for privileged access issues or vulnerabilities. They identify the following accounts by the application:

- AcmeHR

  - High risk

    - WC's Instance DB Administrator

      - This account has the ability to make changes inside the HR database and can create, read, delete, or edit the contents of the database.

    - WC's HR Director

      - This account has the ability to create other administrator accounts as needed in the HR software.

- WC's CEO

  - This is a backup account to create administrator accounts in the HR software if the HR Director is unavailable.

- Medium risk

  - WC's HR Analyst

    - This account has the ability to create new accounts within the HR software as new employees are onboarded.

- Sales-R-Us

  - High risk

    - Database Administrator

      - This role has the ability to delete, edit, and update the data within this sensitive database.

    - Systems Administrator

      - This role has overall control over the database with customer sensitive data.

  - Medium risk

    - Customer Support Representative

      - This role has the ability to view sensitive customer data (credit cards and PII).

- FinanceSW

  - High risk

    - Chief Financial Officer

      - As the lead finance officer for the company, this account has ability to make global changes in the finance software.

    - Senior Financial Analyst

      - This role has the ability to create administrator accounts in the SaaS software.

  - Medium risk

    - Financial Analyst

      - This role has ability to add other users to the finance software for access.

The project team reviewed this list with business owners to ensure the risk for each role is correctly calculated. The risk-based ordering, from high to medium (there was no low risk identified), allowed the team to develop an implementation plan that addressed the highest risks first.

The next step was to develop IAM policies that enforce Privileged Access Management for these three vendors' high-risk roles first. The decision was made to leverage a gateway solution for the vendor Privileged Access Management. The principle here was to create essentially an intermediary box, the gateway, that will manage the privilege access requests to the three high-risk vendor software so the risk can be managed centrally.

Additionally, they determined the steps needed to leverage application programming interface (API) to integrate the PAM gateway into the SIEM and the IDS/IPS systems the Widget Conglomerates uses for its enterprise. They implemented a multifactor authentication system for their vendors and systems for those who use a privileged access role as well as migrating away from passwords to a passkey system with biometrics. This last step, the passkey and biometrics, involved getting the vendors to participate in the development and deployment of the solution to ensure adoption by the third parties. The team worked with security architects to develop a high-level architecture for this solution.

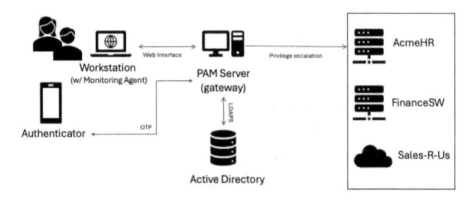

Figure 5-5. *WC Third-Party PAM Architecture*

Once this was all completed, Christian, as the project manager, declared the Planning phase completed and went on to the Execution phase.

Execution

Refresher: The Execution phase takes the hard work done in the first two phases and where changes start to take place in production. Install and configure the chosen PAM implementation across the defined systems for the project. Testing and validation will need to be done on a non-production system and then to the production system to ensure all issues are resolved before onboarding begins. Users can be onboarded using a training process for the updated password management, access requests, and session management changes. There will need to be a period of "Access Remediation" as there often needs to be adjustments to user accounts and policies to get the best practice outcome.

The team decided to take a stepped approach to the deployment of the PAM solution into each of the three vendor solutions. Starting with the Sales-R-Us system, given the risk around customer sensitive data, they implemented the PAM gateway and got the vendor to implement a fingerprint reader on all the systems they utilize for access to Widget C.'s data. The WC team and Sales-R-Us teams agreed to leverage Microsoft's Authenticator for the MFA as they are both heavy users of Microsoft systems. The testing began with the database administrator role, and they set the just-in-time permissions to be no more than two hours before a time-out is forced and the database administrator has to be reauthenticated and a new token issued. Next up was the system administrator role being integrated and tested into the PAM gateway and onto the Sales-R-Us application.

The team took on the FinanceSW vendor access risks next by integrating and testing the two high-risk identities in this system. Given that the Chief Financial Officer was one of the high-risk roles and these C-level employees are typically not the most patient of types, there was a need to ensure the steps for authentication, authorization, and entitlements were as seamless as possible with as few as steps as needed. The testing ensured that the CFO would have a trouble-free experience when they needed to perform administrative functions. More importantly, they created a "normal" user account for the CFO that only had viewing rights for the data to allow that role to see data without fear of changing or altering it. This was the role the CFO was encouraged to log in with, and to further "encourage" this, the privileged access role was only given one hour of just-in-time access.

The next steps was to get the AcmeHR privileged access roles integrated and tested into the PAM system. Similar to the CFO, the HR Director was determined to be in a role that would likely have challenges if the PAM process was too cumbersome. This meant treating it the same way and providing the HR Director with a "normal" user role they would log in with on their day-to-day work to ensure they are not doing administrative work accidentally. Lastly, they tested the CFO experience as well to find out if the role could be accomplished with little support or guidance if needed.

Governance

As the team builds out the program, there must be an effort to build the governance framework around the PAM deployment and program. Much of the foundational work for IAM and PAM deployment was already in their policy and procedure documentation. The changes required were focused mainly on folding in the new steps for the new PAM gateway and the process for Privileged Access Management and life cycle.

Because they centralized the vendor access into a PAM gateway, this meant that only one process document had to be created; they just had to add three "flavors" for each of the three applications that were involved. The ideal way to develop the procedure documentation was to have the project manager work with a business analyst to document the process for each of the roles into each of the systems and then spend time reviewing those processes with the owners to check for accuracy and any potential issues. Once the procedures were documented, reviewed, and re-run to validate accuracy, they were sent to the owners for each of the applications and the IAM leader, Kristina, for their review and approval. The procedure document was given a version control section that listed these approvers, their signatures, and when it was approved and was set to be re-reviewed and approved again in a year from that date.

Widget C. has a policy document control software that centrally manages and stores all policy and procedure documents. When the PAM procedure document was finalized, it was uploaded into the document control tool, and then, an announcement was sent company-wide to this new procedure document, what was its scope, who approved it, and when it is up for review and approval in the future.

Root Cause Analysis

During the Execution phase, there will be a need to find why things are not working correctly. There are a thousand different types of issues that can happen, and the type of issue that is encountered is less important than what your team decides to do with it. Does the team spend time fixing the symptom or the root cause? It is easy and very typical for a IAM team to fix an individual PAM account issue and not look to find out why the issue came up in the first place. The idea is to prevent the issue from happening in the first place (again) and thus removing the fault entirely.

Root cause analysis (RCA) is the process of discovering the root causes of problems in order to identify appropriate solutions. RCA assumes that it is much more effective to systematically prevent and solve for underlying issues rather than just treating ad hoc symptoms and putting out fires. There are a number of types of methods to perform RCA.

Root cause analysis techniques are systematic methods used to identify the underlying causes of a problem by examining potential factors and systematically drilling down to pinpoint the most significant contributors, allowing for targeted solutions rather than just treating symptoms; common techniques include the five whys, fishbone diagrams (Ishikawa diagrams), Pareto analysis, and change analysis. We will use the fault tree analysis for the purpose of this exercise to demonstrate an example of RCA in the PAM deployment and implementation.

Fault tree analysis is a top-down and deductive failure analysis technique that allows the team to graphically map the possible causes for failure. FTA is a systematic method used to identify potential causes of a specific undesired event within a complex system by working backward from the "top event" (the undesirable outcome), breaking down the possible failure paths into smaller, more manageable events, ultimately revealing the root causes that could lead to the top event, essentially creating a visual diagram that resembles a tree, with each branch representing a potential failure sequence.

Example:

During deployment, there is a recurring event where privileged users in the FinanceSW system were dropped from the PAM gateway and thus had to be manually re-entered. The non-RCA method was to simply keep adding these users back into the system manually. That was determined to be the stop-gap fix, while the root cause analysis team got together to determine what it is. The team got together and started doing a fault tree analysis for the error.

Key components of a login failure fault tree:

- Top event: "Login unsuccessful"

Branches (potential causes):

- Invalid credentials
    - Incorrect username
    - Incorrect password
    - Case sensitivity issues
    - Typos

- Authentication issues
    - Server unavailable
    - Database connectivity problems
    - Authentication service failure
    - Session timeout

- User interface problems

  - Login form errors

  - Missing fields

  - Unclear error messages

  - Responsive design issues

- Network issues

  - Network connectivity loss

  - Slow network speed

  - Firewall blocking access

- Security measures

  - Two-factor authentication failure

  - Captcha recognition errors

  - Password complexity requirements not met

The team went down each of these potential issues causes and assigned owners to investigate. After a few days of investigation, it was discovered that the PAM gateway server was unavailable at midnight to 1 am while the system was performing a backup. The team determined that the users were trying to perform work during this window. During this window, the system did not recognize them as a privileged user and so the users would then request a new privileged account or re-enable their existing one. The decision was made to create a secondary PAM gateway that would act both as a redundant backup for the primary, but also traffic would be directed to this secondary when backups were occurring. This eliminated the problem from occurring again, and the issue was marked as resolved.

Closure

Refresher: The Closure phase involves closing out the project to ensure all the deliverables, within the defined scope, are completed and the key stakeholders have signed off on it. Once all the deliverables have been agreed as completed, there should be a post-implementation evaluation to analyze the effectiveness of both the project team and the project outcomes. In addition, one of the most important checklist items on this phase is the "turning over" operation from the project team to the IAM and/or PAM team that will manage this day-to-day.

The project team completed the implementation of the PAM solution to all three vendors successfully. This was determined by the project manager taking all the deliverables and scope statement to the key stakeholders. These artifacts and facts were reviewed by this group, and once agreed, they all approved the completion of the project with an acknowledgment email stating that fact. All the project artifacts were stored in the appropriate place on the company intranet, and the project manager was assigned to another project in the pipeline. The next project was determined to be the next identified risk for privileged access systems at Widget C. Lastly, the project team met with the IAM team to formalize the conversion from a project to operations.

Operationalize

Once the project to implement PAM for the three vendors was completed, the last step was to meet with the IAM team to formalize the handoff to that team. This will operationalize the process and make it part of their normal, day-to-day operations. Governance documentation was reviewed and confirmed to be accurate. There was a formal email sent from the project team that the IAM leader acknowledged the "acceptance" of the project into their queue as normal business operations they will handle going forward.

Metrics for Success

The best metrics for any program are Key Performance Indicators (KPIs) or Key Risk Indicators (KRIs). As the team worked with the IAM team, the CISO, and Chief Risk Officer (CRO), they determined which of the existing KPIs could be utilized and any new KPI or KRI that needed to be added for this new control.

1. Session Monitoring: Monitoring sessions is a key measurement to observe the real-time use of privileged accounts. This measurement is useful to detect unauthorized activities and ensure elevated users are following the policy and process. The IAM team ensured that the advanced monitoring tools were enabled to log all privileged sessions and that escalation procedures were listed in the governance documentation.

2. Ownership and Accountability: This measures the owners and accountable for privileged accounts and helps simplify the audit trail for forensics if needed. This KPI will ensure every privileged account has an assigned owner or team, along with verifying that account owners are aware of this privileged account, what responsibilities that entails, and roles that get updated with changes in personnel.

3. Access Reviews: As told many times, access reviews are a key control in any IAM enterprise system. This KPI evaluates how often WC reviews privileged accounts and ensures the roles are correctly matched. It ensures that WC is following the published access reviews for these accounts per the governance documentation.

4. Unauthorized Access Attempts: Focused on privileged accounts, this KPI will list the number of attempts to login at this level unsuccessfully.

5. Use Patterns: The KPI will look for anomalous behavior by looking at usage patterns and compare against regular patterns observed. The team had to connect this KPI with the User Behavior Analytics engine to get accurate information.

6. Compliance: Because the Widget C. stores sensitive customer data and sells in California, it knows it was subject to reporting requirements around the California privacy regulations. The team connected those requirements to the PAM system to determine if there is any deviation.

7. Inventory Management: Knowing all the assets at the WC enterprise is critical to ensure all potential access points are known. The team leverages this KPI to look for any asset or services that should be part of the PAM solution but have escaped the onboarding process.

The process to implement a Privileged Access Management program and process at any enterprise is best done in iterations. The example provided shows how Widget Conglomerates chose to do its vendor PAM problem first. If WC were a real company we worked for, the next logical step would be to identify the next, best (risk-order) target to implement into the PAM program and tackle it. Then, identify the next target, and repeat. Improve the project and process as your team learns lessons and gets feedback.

PAM for IoT

The Internet of Things (IoT) is not new and describes a set a broad category of electronic items that are connected to the Internet. They range from webcams and treadmills to security cameras and building control systems. IoT comes from British scientist Kevin Ashton in 1999, who coined the phrase "the Internet of Things" to reflect the expanding collection of electronic devices connecting to each other over the Internet.[4] The number has grown far beyond what Ashton probably ever imagined and is expected to be 24.1 billion IoT devices by 2030.[5]

These devices often have built-in, hard-coded username and password credentials. These IoT devices, once compromised, can have malware installed on them, or they can be hijacked and controlled by the bad actors. Many of these devices are now crucial to operations, and so, securing these devices and their elevated accounts is critical.

Privileged access management programs must continually discover and onboard new devices and elevated accounts or roles when added to your enterprise. These accounts and users must be steered away from default passwords most importantly. These IoT devices can be challenging to onboard, but most modern solutions will be able to bring these devices into the system, control them, rotate credentials, and ensure unauthorized access is prevented. Additionally, there are PAM solutions that can work with gateways to control access to these devices that would be secured in a bastion.

Implement endpoint security on these devices where possible. This can be accomplished by an endpoint privilege manager (EPM) to strengthen these systems to maintain firm privilege security, enforcing least privilege, and reduce the risk of unauthorized access. Many of the IoT devices will allow for remote access, and it is crucial to enable remote

---

[4] https://www.britannica.com/science/Internet-of-Things
[5] https://cisomag.com/number-of-iot-devices-expected-to-reach-24-1-bn-in-2030-report/

access security with Privileged Access Management solution. Secure remote access is best done through a gateway to better manage access into these IoT systems. Rotate the credentials based upon your organizational policies and procedures.

One of the keys to success in this space is to do your best to think like a bad actor. One thing bad actors will never tire of doing is the simplest of ways to get into an IoT system: use the paperclip to reset the device. Most of these devices will have a push button that is activated with a small metal pushpin like a paperclip that resets the device back to default username and passwords. These devices must be monitored for this type of action, and when detected, the PAM solution should automatically (or suggest how) rotate the credentials and investigate the logs for any clues to an event, incident, or breach. Another method for securing these devices is to use a unidirectional gateway (sometimes called a data diode) to integrate with your PAM solution.

Highly Regulated Environments

Highly regulated environments are ones that have a large number of regulatory oversight bodies and can be federal, state, or local level. The examples of highly regulated industries are healthcare, insurance, pharmaceuticals, energy, finance, telecommunications, alcohol, tobacco, and automobiles. There are likely more than this list, and if you are unsure, inquire with your legal and/or compliance teams. Highly regulated companies are often subject to more stringent data protection and incident reporting requirements.

While the principles of Privileged Access Management and Zero Trust do not vary in these types of industries, there are additional concerns with compliance and reporting that should be addressed. The NIST and National Cybersecurity Center of Excellence have published an excellent guide

"Privileged Account Management for the Financial Services."[6] While this example is not the answer for all highly regulated industries, it can provide adequate guidance on what's most important in these organizations.

The biggest challenge in these industries is compliance. Compliance is the state of being within the guidance of policy, procedure, or guidelines. Compliance indicates whether a company adheres to the applicable laws, rules, and regulations in their industry. Identify these compliance requirements within your industry, and ensure your PAM solution and program provide the details for the various lines of defense who will oversee and evaluate the program.

Third-Party Access

Third parties are organizations we deal with almost continually at our enterprise. These are vendors, but the term third party includes any external party (partner, supplier, vendor) but not customers or clients. No company wants to solve for all of its challenges. A bank does not want to make human resources software, and a software company does not want to make its own server hardware to load its software onto. Every company and organization on this planet has at least one third party helping it perform critical functions. Example scenarios:

- A Cloud Service Provider needing temporary access to manage your cloud infrastructure

- A software vendor requiring privileged access to troubleshoot issues on your internal systems

- A network maintenance contractor needing elevated permissions to configure network devices

---

[6] https://www.nccoe.nist.gov/financial-services/privileged-account-management

Most organizations have hundreds to thousands of third parties that keep them operating on a daily basis. Think of third parties as extensions of your enterprise, and that is the way to think of how to manage their risk to your organization. Vendor Privileged Access Management (VPAM) is a term used in this space.

In this spirit, there is little difference to how an organization would treat their own internal users who have a privileged account vs. a vendor with a privileged account. The functionality and principles are the same for PAM across these two types of users (internal and vendor). Least privilege, just-in-time access, session monitoring, and strong authentication are areas to lean in very heavily on the vendor privileged accounts.

The most common way to solve for the risk around VPAM is to leverage a web portal (much like described in the sample implementation described above in this chapter). This web portal precludes the vendor logging directly into the system in question but allows this risk to be isolated, controlled, and audited in a central location. In addition, because vendor users are not your users, there is a sense of the "unknown" for them, and it would be best practice to leverage more robust authentication processes such as a passkey and biometric login measures.

Best Practices and Pitfalls

Along with all the above provided for how to have a successful PAM implementation, there are three more items that are crucial to success. Getting buy-in and support from your leadership for a PAM deployment is a critical first step to any large project like this that has a wide and large impact. Next is the issues around "discovery" of privileged accounts and roles and how best to accomplish. Lastly, and related to the discovery piece, is to allow for "out of scope" systems that may not be able (or willing, due to business reasons) to convert into the PAM ecosystem.

Leadership Support

A Privileged Access Management project and program is going to cut across many business teams and areas within most organizations. While your team likely thinks that deploying a PAM solution is a great idea, it will take some convincing of other impacted groups to share that feeling. In order to make their acceptance of this new reality more appealing, getting your leadership onboard and supportive is critical. It isn't that you're going to tell the folks who are reluctant that you're going to tell the leadership if they don't cooperate, but it is more about having them adopt a PAM strategy, and that enables your team the ability to accomplish the tactical steps to be successful.

One of the best ways to get leadership support is to make the business case for Privileged Access Management. There are a variety of ways that an organization can get a return on investment (ROI) for a PAM deployment. The first is password vaulting. Passwords are the weakest link in the chain of security for most enterprises.[7] The most used passwords are still "Password" and "Secret" or variations of them (P@ssw0rd, or S3cr3t, for example). Folks still write down passwords on paper or store them in a password-protected spreadsheet. In a password vault, the credentials are stored in a safe, digital, encrypted location that is governed by your access control policies. This means you can make more complex passwords that are more challenging to crack and not overtax the user base.

Automating passwords is another key benefit of deploying a PAM solution. Asking users to create complex, long passwords usually means they do not or they cheat and write them down or reuse them across multiple platforms. None of these are good outcomes. Automating the creation of complex, hard to break passwords takes the guesswork out of it for the end users and assures the IAM team that they are getting the complexity they require.

---

[7] https://www.wsj.com/tech/cybersecurity/passwords-proposed-new-federal-guidelines-2ba177d8?mod=saved_content

The other upside selling point of PAM is the ability to manage nonhuman accounts. Most organizations tend to focus on roles and accounts used by humans such as administrators, developers, vendors, and C-level staff. This is natural with the focus on insider threats, whether it is intentional or accidental. Much of the risk though still lies with these machine or service accounts with privileged access. Often these accounts are not required to perform PAM process because leadership is scared to touch them. It is not uncommon for those examining these types of accounts to find that they've not had a password change in years—again because staff is afraid of the consequences if they are changed. The PAM solution will get these accounts under management and, thus, under control. This will drastically reduce this (often) unrealized risk.

Next, a vendor PAM (VPAM) has a huge benefit to any organization. There is plenty of data around the risk for third parties to enterprises, but the simplest one to know is that 98% of organizations report doing business with a vendor who has had a breach in the last two years. That is close enough to 100% to call it 100% for most folks. This statistic means nearly every organization is doing business with a third party that has been breached. This results in the assertion that a third-party breach is inevitable for most organizations. Not a question of if, but when. Getting these risky vendor elevated accounts under a PAM program will greatly reduce this risk in this domain.

Lastly, the deployment of a PAM solution is key to a Zero Trust deployment. Many organizations are readying or in the process of deploying Zero Trust. PAM establishes a Zero Trust framework because it requires continuous verification of all the enterprise's passwords, privileged accounts, and secrets. The Zero Trust framework provides the organization a full visibility into the privileged account activity and all users and devices. PAM enforces least-privileged access that is key to Zero Trust success. It eliminates unneeded privileges that can be exploited by bad actors and automates the configuration of privileged accounts. Automating the configuration of privileged accounts and performing continuous monitoring, access management, and reporting are all outcomes from PAM that are needed for a Zero Trust strategy.

As you look to get buy-in and support for a Privileged Access Management program in your enterprise, look to get support from the leaders within your organization first. Then, look to leverage their support and your facts with leaders from any other leaders in business units impacted or included. These leaders will be your key stakeholders (or their delegates) when the project kicks off.

Complete Discovery

One of the most important steps in the deployment of PAM is ensuring the complete discovery of all privileged accounts. Let's start by stating that this is an ongoing affair and not expected to be done on a single run. This is a continuous effort and never is really completed, but during a project to deploy PAM in an environment, it is important to get as much of 100% as is possible. There are ways to help lower the number of accounts missed with some simple rules and tips to follow.

Many PAM technologies and tools come with an "auto-discovery" tool that can be leveraged. This is excellent to use, and there is nothing wrong with leveraging this built-in functionality. However, it would not be sufficient to rely solely on the tool or technology—always look for other ways that might be missed. First, look at the asset inventory database (CMDB) to determine if all assets are accounted for in the space you're deploying PAM. This technique identifies every asset in the enterprise and provides details on users, services, applications, vulnerabilities, operating systems, and more. This information is then correlated to help the team classify assets and accounts based upon sensitivity, data, ownership, location, and users.

As you look to deploy PAM solutions to assets, there is a common piece: that they require a credential to be managed, and that credential can be retrieved using a comprehensive discovery solution within the PAM tool or another commercial off-the-shelf tool. Most of these tools will allow a listing of privileged accounts, privileges associated with it, and their group membership. This listing will provide you with nearly all of the accounts needed in the PAM deployment.

Compare the list of privileged account types below with what your organization has discovered, and list any that might need to be manually found.

- Domain administrator accounts

- Domain service accounts

- Local administrator accounts

- Machine accounts

- Service accounts

- Management solutions

- Application accounts

- Embedded credentials

Allow for "Out of Scope"

There are instances in the real world where a role or account will need privileged access for a system typically "out of scope" for their job function. A great example would be a network administrator who typically manages routers and switches is called in to troubleshoot a problem with latency issues connecting to a database. In the course of troubleshooting the issue, the network administrator requests access to the database to discover if the latency is at the database end, not the network. This will require the network administrator to request an "out of scope" access level to connect to the database and troubleshoot the latency issue. It seemingly breaks the "least privilege" rule giving these permissions since the network administrator doesn't have the role of database administrator.

When allowing for the "out of scope," there needs to be some rules around when and how it is allowed. The first step is to limit the access to ensure only the permissions required are given to this access. Don't default to giving them root-level access, while that is certainly the "easy button" option, it definitely breaks the least-privilege rule. Ensure that your IAM and PAM governance documentation accounts for a process to get this approval and that it requires a strict approval process. These access requests must be approved by an appropriate level of authority to match the risk level. The requests must be time-bound and preferably auto-revoked when the time runs out. Ensure there is strong authentication, multifactor authentication, clearly defined use cases for submission, and a strong justification process for request. Lastly, all these "out of scope" access requests and attempts must be logged and monitored to determine if anything malicious is occurring.

Chapter Summary

This chapter focused on how to best implement a Privileged Access Management solution.

- Project Management Methodologies: Incorporate project management methodologies specific to how to deploy PAM.

- Stakeholder Management: Discuss strategies for managing various stakeholders during implementation.

- Plan of Action:

  - Planning

  - Execution

  - Governance

  - Root cause analysis

  - Operationalize

  - Metrics for success

- PAM in DevOps: Discuss the role of PAM in DevOps environments.

- Human vs. Machine Access: Break down how PAM/ZT needs to work for human-to-machine access vs. machine-to-machine access. Tie back to identity management (person vs. machine identity).

- Tools and Technologies: There are a lot technologies around PAM, and we will provide some ways to sort through the jargon and fancy bells and whistles to determine the best fit for your organization.

- PAM for IoT: Explore the challenges and solutions for managing privileged access in IoT and other emerging tech.

- Heavily Regulated: Address sector-specific challenges and solutions in PAM implementation.

- Third-Party Access: Discuss the risks and best ways to lower the risk of vendor Privileged Access Management.

- Best Practices and Pitfalls: Share best practices and common pitfalls across different scenarios.

CHAPTER 6

Conclusion

Chapter Overview

- Building a Learning Organization: Talk about how organizations can continuously adapt to evolving security landscapes

- Resource Compendium: Offer a comprehensive list of resources.

- Book Summary: A final wrap of all the topics covered to assist the reader with boiling it down.

Building a Learning Organization

Cybersecurity is an ongoing effort that never ends. The bad actors never stop trying and devising new methods to exploit vulnerabilities. One of the most significant vulnerabilities is humans in the enterprise. Even though we built these organizations for the benefit of humans, they continue to do things like choosing terrible, easy-to-guess passwords and finding ways to circumvent security controls. In addition to using preventive and detective

© Gregory C. Rasner, Maria C. Rasner 2025
G. C. Rasner and M. C. Rasner, *Privileged Access Management*,
https://doi.org/10.1007/979-8-8688-1431-0_6

controls, education is one of the best ways to reduce the risk posed by humans. Teach users why and how to behave, and most will comply. However, building a learning organization is often overlooked completely or not fully invested in and thorough.

First, a learning organization must have a leader for learning. This requires a learning program that is funded and supported by senior leadership. There is a life cycle for how a learning program operates. This lifecycle can be seen in the figure below:

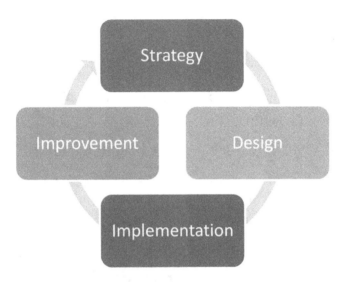

Figure 6-1. *Learning Program Life Cycle*

Strategy

Like any large endeavor, a strategy must be developed first for success. Strategy statements will vary, but let's start with a sample for use:

"Our user training strategy will prioritize proactive, accessible, and tailored learning experiences to empower users of all levels with the necessary skills to fully utilize our platform, focusing on core functionalities through a blended approach of interactive online modules, targeted in-person workshops, and readily available support resources, ultimately driving high adoption rates and maximizing user satisfaction."

Strategy is discussed in some detail by the NIST SP 800-50r1 in Section 2.1 "Building the Strategic Plan." The recommendation is to develop a strategy that builds on the organization's plan for continuous worker development. The owner of the training program must understand the structure and mission of the company to comprehend how the strategy originates. The strategy must be clearly stated and agreed upon by leadership before work begins:

- **Support culture**

  Ensure the plan supports the culture of a risk-based, decision-making one that understands the importance of learning, to include the development of new skills and refresher of existing skills best practices.

- **Measure gaps**

  How will the program meet the knowledge and skills gaps that have been identified and enhance skills and capabilities of the enterprise.

- **Focus on user needs**

  The primary goal is to equip users with the knowledge and skills they need to effectively use the platform, addressing different levels of expertise.

- **Blended learning approach**

  Combining online modules for self-paced learning with in-person workshops for hands-on practice and clarification.

- **Accessibility**

  Ensuring training materials and delivery methods are readily available to all users, regardless of location or technical proficiency.

- **Tailored content**

  Customizing training pathways based on user roles and specific needs to maximize relevance and impact.

- **Measurable outcome**

  High adoption rates and user satisfaction are key indicators of a successful training strategy. Include metrics and measures that will help determine if the current programs are meeting goals. Ensure that success can be measured in substantive terms and not on nonmeasurable goals.

Design

When designing user education for cybersecurity, you can consider the following:

- Format: Make the information easy to understand and focus on the most important details.

- Length: Keep the training brief.

- Interactivity: Use interactive tutorials or gamification to make the training more engaging.

- UX Design: Apply effective design principles to create intuitive and visually appealing interfaces.

- Feedback: Provide meaningful feedback, such as notifications or alerts, to help users understand the consequences of their actions.

- Customization: Tailor the training to suit the audience's role, learning styles, and preferred media.

- Frequency: Conduct regular training sessions and refreshers to keep users informed.

- Security Fundamentals: Provide a core set of terms, topics, and concepts to build upon.

- Training and Awareness: Training should impart skills, while awareness should address specific issues.

As the design of the program takes shape, ensure that you adopt a risk-based approach to its implementation.

Implementation

As your designs for training take shape, there should be a phased approach to implementation. Look for quick wins initially to learn how to implement successfully. Adopt a project approach and have a project manager oversee the effort so the scope, schedule, budget, and resources are properly managed and aligned. Identify steps or milestones along the way to assess success and seek opportunities for improvement.

Improvement

Like all processes, the training program is never perfect and will always seek continuous improvement. Regularly evaluate progress and adjust the training program as needed. This is best achieved by reviewing evaluation results alongside outcomes in the enterprise. For example, if you have a Privileged Access Management training for administrators and there are good passing numbers on the assessment at the end of the training for these administrators, yet the organization is still experiencing accounts that are not being onboarded and/or seeing administrators working around the system, this means you might need to change your training.

Some key considerations for leaders developing a learning environment are detailed in the National Institute of Standards and Technology Special Publication 800-50r1, updated in September 2024:

- Develop, maintain, and implement mandatory organization-wide training for all workforce members that supports enterprise cybersecurity and privacy goals and objectives.

- Ensure all training aligns with established rules of behavior and is consistent with applicable policies, standards, and guidelines.

- Notify the workforce about available cybersecurity and privacy resources, including policies, products, techniques, best practices, and expertise.

- Provide foundational and advanced levels of cybersecurity and privacy training to the workforce, and ensure measures are in place to assess participants' knowledge and skills.

- In consultation with senior leadership, identify cybersecurity and privacy behaviors that impact risk in a data-driven manner.

- Identify those who need specialized cybersecurity and privacy training based on assigned cybersecurity and privacy roles and responsibilities.

- Measure attitudes, behaviors, and workforce sentiment as part of tracking the development of a cybersecurity and privacy culture.

- Leading by example and participating in their own CPLP training, as required.

- Identifying individuals responsible for cybersecurity and privacy and documenting these responsibilities in position descriptions or other relevant work and performance requirement statements.

- Identifying relevant learning requirements and documenting them in individual development plans or other career pathway documentation.

- Establishing policies and procedures for learning programs and documenting them in organizational records.

- If serving as the system owner or data owner, designate staff who have significant cybersecurity and/or privacy responsibilities for their system (e.g., general support systems and major applications), and ensure that users and support personnel are appropriately trained on how to fulfill their responsibilities before being granted access to system resources.[1]

Building a learning culture—one where gaps and issues are addressed with education that is welcomed and absorbed—takes a concerted effort. It does not just "happen" organically. If left unattended, users will educate themselves in ways that likely run counter to your organization's desired outcomes. Building a learning organization will create an entity that is less risky and more productive.

---

[1] https://nvlpubs.nist.gov/nistpubs/SpecialPublications/NIST. SP.800-50r1.pdf

Resource Compendium

There are many resources on the Privileged Access Management and Zero Trust challenges. Some of the resources were used extensively for this book and are great resources for practitioners and leaders in both domains. We will group some of the resources into logical sections for easier use and provide some explanation of the perceived benefits for PAM and ZT.

- National Institute of Standards and Technology Small Business Cybersecurity Webinar: Identity and Access Management Fundamentals for Small Business: `https://www.nist.gov/system/files/documents/2024/10/23/10.23-SMB%20IdAM.pdf`

- National Institute of Standards and Technology Cybersecurity Framework 2.0: Small Business Quick-Start Guide: `https://nvlpubs.nist.gov/nistpubs/SpecialPublications/NIST.SP.1300.pdf`

- National Institute of Standards and Technology Small Business Cybersecurity Corner: Choosing a (Cybersecurity) Vendor or Service Provider: `https://www.nist.gov/itl/smallbusinesscyber/guidance-topic/choosing-vendorservice-provider`

- Federal Communication Commission Cybersecurity for Small Businesses: `https://www.fcc.gov/communications-business-opportunities/cybersecurity-small-businesses`

- The GCA Cybersecurity Toolkit for Small Business: `https://gcatoolkit.org/smallbusiness/`

- Federal Trade Commission Cybersecurity for Small Business: `https://www.ftc.gov/business-guidance/small-businesses/cybersecurity`

- National Cybersecurity Alliance: `https://staysafeonline.org`

- NISTIR 7621 Small Business Information Security: The Fundamentals: `https://www.govinfo.gov/content/pkg/GOVPUB-C13-7bad944538579c44b5b3ba35f2f b8f13/pdf/GOVPUB-C13-7bad944538579c44b5b3ba35f2 fb8f13.pdf`

- Building a Cybersecurity and Privacy Learning Program (NIST SP 800-50r1): `https://nvlpubs.nist.gov/nistpubs/SpecialPublications/NIST.SP.800-50r1.pdf`

- Digital Identity Guidelines (National Institute of Standards and Technology SP 800-63-4): `https://csrc.nist.gov/pubs/sp/800/63/4/2pd`

- National Institute of Standards and Technology Small Business Security MFA Fact Sheet: `https://www.nist.gov/system/files/documents/2024/02/15/MFA-SMB_2024_Final.pdf`

- Security and Privacy Controls for Information Systems and Organizations: `https://nvlpubs.nist.gov/nistpubs/SpecialPublications/NIST.SP.800-53r5.pdf`

- National Institute of Standards and Technology Definition of Privileged User: `https://csrc.nist.gov/glossary/term/privileged_user`

- National Institute of Standards and Technology and National Cybersecurity Center of Excellence Privileged Account Management Use Case I Financial Services: https://www.nccoe.nist.gov/sites/default/files/legacy-files/fs-pam-fact-sheet.pdf

- "Zero Trust Security: An Enterprise Guide": Apress Publishing, Jason Garbis, Jerry W. Chapman, 2021

- The President's National Security Telecommunications Advisory Committee Report to the President: Zero Trust and Trust Identity Management (Feb 2023): https://www.cisa.gov/sites/default/files/publications/NSTAC%20Report%20to%20the%20President%20on%20Zero%20Trust%20and%20Trusted%20Identity%20Management.pdf

- "No More Chewy Centers: Introducing the Zero Trust Model of Information Security" by John Kindervag: https://media.paloaltonetworks.com/documents/Forrester-No-More-Chewy-Centers.pdf

- National Institute of Standards and Technology SP 800-207: Zero Trust Architecture: https://csrc.nist.gov/publications/detail/sp/800-207/final

- Executive Order on Improving the Nation's Cybersecurity: https://www.whitehouse.gov/briefing-room/presidential-actions/2021/05/12/executive-order-on-improving-the-nations-cybersecurity

- Office of Management and Budget, M-22-09: Moving the U.S. Government Toward Zero Trust Cybersecurity Principles, The White House, January 26, 2022: https://www.whitehouse.gov/wp-content/uploads/2022/01/M-22-09.pdf

- Defining the Zero Trust Protect Surface, CSA: `https://cloudsecurityalliance.org/artifacts/defining-the-zero-trust-protect-surface`

- Implementing a Zero Trust Architecture (National Institute of Standards and Technology and National Cybersecurity Center of Excellence): `https://www.nccoe.nist.gov/projects/implementing-zero-trust-architecture`

- National Cyber Security Centre, Device Security Guidance, Network Architectures: `https://www.ncsc.gov.uk/collection/device-security-guidance/infrastructure/network-architectures`

- Zero Trust Maturity Model (v. 2.0), Cybersecurity Infrastucture Security Agency: `https://www.cisa.gov/sites/default/files/2023-04/zero_trust_maturity_model_v2_508.pdf`

- National Institute of Standards and Technology SP 800-207: Zero Trust Architecture: `https://nvlpubs.nist.gov/nistpubs/SpecialPublications/NIST.SP.800-207.pdf`

- National Security Agency Cybersecurity Information Sheet: Managing Risk from Software Defined Networking Controllers: `https://media.defense.gov/2023/Dec/12/2003357491/-1/-1/0/CSI_MANAGING_RISK_FROM_SDN_CONTROLLERS.PDF`

- National Institute of Standards and Technology SP 1800-35: Implementing a Zero Trust Architecture: High-Level Document: `https://www.nccoe.nist.gov/sites/default/files/2024-07/zta-nist-sp-1800-35-preliminary-draft-4.pdf`

- National Institute of Standards and Technology Definition of a Policy Enforcement Point: https://csrc.nist.gov/glossary/term/policy_enforcement_point

- What Is Zero Trust Security (CSA): https://cloudsecurityalliance.org/blog/2023/09/29/what-are-the-main-concepts-of-zero-trust

- U.S. Department of Homeland Security, Cybersecurity Strategy: https://www.dhs.gov/sites/default/files/publications/DHS-Cybersecurity-Fact-Sheet.pdf

- Cybersecurity Infrastucture Security Agency's Cyber Security Strategic Plan: https://www.dhs.gov/sites/default/files/publications/DHS-Cybersecurity-Strategy_1.pdf

- State of Vermont Cybersecurity Strategy: https://digitalservices.vermont.gov/sites/digitalservices/files/doc_library/Cybersecurity-Strategy.pdf

- National Institute of Standards and Technology Cybersecurity Framework (NIST-CSF) 2.0 Informative References: https://www.nist.gov/informative-references

- National Institute of Standards and Technology CSF 2.0 Landing Page: https://www.nist.gov/cyberframework

- NISTIR 7621 R1, Small Business Information Security: The Fundamentals: https://nvlpubs.nist.gov/nistpubs/ir/2016/nist.ir.7621r1.pdf

- National Institute of Standards and Technology Small Business Cybersecurity Corner: `https://www.nist.gov/itl/smallbusinesscyber`

- National Institute of Standards and Technology Cybersecurity Framework 2.0: Small Business Quick-Start Guide: `https://nvlpubs.nist.gov/nistpubs/SpecialPublications/NIST.SP.1300.pdf`

- National Institute of Standards and Technology Risk Management Framework: `https://csrc.nist.gov/Projects/risk-management/about-rmf/assess-step`

- National Institute of Standards and Technology Cybersecurity Framework Policy Template Guide: `https://www.cisecurity.org/-/jssmedia/Project/cisecurity/cisecurity/data/media/img/uploads/2021/11/NIST-Cybersecurity-Framework-Policy-Template-Guide-v2111Online.pdf`

- National Institute of Standards and Technology Small Business Cybersecurity Corner: Choosing a Vendor/Service Provider: `https://www.nist.gov/itl/smallbusinesscyber/guidance-topic/choosing-vendorservice-provider`

- Cyber Readiness Institute "Should I Get Outside Support to Manage My Cybersecurity Risk": `https://cyberreadinessinstitute.org/resource/should-i-get-outside-support-to-manage-my-cybersecurity-risk/`

- Cybersecurity Infrastucture Security Agency's List of Critical Infrastructure Sectors: `https://www.cisa.gov/topics/critical-infrastructure-security-and-resilience/critical-infrastructure-sectors`

- SANS Security Policy Templates: `https://www.sans.org/information-security-policy/?per-page=100`

- Cybersecurity Infrastucture Security Agency's Policy Templates: `https://www.cisecurity.org/controls/policy-templates`

- Center for Internet Security Critical Security Controls v8.1: `https://learn.cisecurity.org/cis-controls-download?_gl=1*1pmbdyd*_gcl_aw*RONMLjE3MzQxOTM1O DAuQ2p3SONBaUE5dlM2QmhBOUVpdOFKcG5Yd3hkbHRI ZnlUTmNCcDhCUUw1bVR3YU1aWUdwanNtWndyNWpKcDFK RTJiRGN4RO1BMENFZW5obONyVzhRQXZEXOJ3RQ.. *_gcl_au*Mjg4MjE3NTA1LjE3MzQxOTM1NzE.*_ga* MTEwNDY4NDY5Mi4xNzMOMTkzNTY4*_ga_N7OZ2MK MD7*MTczNDE5MzU2Ny4xLjEuMTczNDE5MzY5MC4xOC4 wLjA.*_ga_3FW1B1JC98*MTczNDE5MzU2Ny4xLjEuMTcz NDE5MzY5MC4wLjAuMA`

- Virginia IT Agency IT Security Policy and Procedure Templates: `https://www.vita.virginia.gov/policy--governance/policies-standards--guidelines/it-security-policy--procedure-templates/`

- Privileged Account Management for the Financial Services Sector: `https://www.nccoe.nist.gov/sites/default/files/legacy-files/fs-pam-nist-sp1800-18-draft.pdf`

- Google PAM Overview: `https://cloud.google.com/iam/docs/pam-overview`

- Amazon PAM Overview: `https://aws.amazon.com/blogs/security/temporary-elevated-access-management-with-iam-identity-center/`

- National Institute of Standards and Technology SP
  800-50r1 Building a Cybersecurity and Privacy Learning
  Program: `https://nvlpubs.nist.gov/nistpubs/`
  `SpecialPublications/NIST.SP.800-50r1.pdf`

While these are in chapter order to a large degree, the resources
leveraged and cited above for the book are great assets for further use. The
truth is there is a lot of information already out in the Web for Privileged
Access Management; the trick is consolidating it into a single source of
truth for practitioners.

Chapter Summary

This chapter provides for two large deliverables: how to build on the
success of a PAM deployment by building a learning organization that will
continue to improve and learn. The second is a list of resources online
for readers to utilize on their own for more help on Privileged Access
Management and Zero Trust. The list is long, and as indicated, there is a lot
of information already available for use.

Book Summary

The book is done, and this is a chance to summarize what has been
covered for the readers:

Part I: The Fundamentals

- Chapter 1: Privileged Access Management: The
  Essentials

  - An overview of Privileged Access Management
    (PAM) to ensure all readers are on the same page
    as we dive into this topic much more profoundly.

We defined a privileged account as "a user that is authorized (and therefore, trusted) to perform security-relevant functions that ordinary users are not authorized to perform."[2] Several types of typical elevated accounts exist, such as service accounts, domain administrators, and application administrators.

- The four steps for successful PAM implementation are as follows:

  - Discovery

  - Governance

  - Monitor and audit

  - Automate

- The four steps of a successful PAM life cycle are as follows:

  - Define and Discover

  - Onboarding

  - Monitor and Audit

  - Offboarding

- These are the Magnificent Seven PAM Best Practices:

  - Enforce MFA

  - Cross-platform support

  - Temporary elevated access (TEA)

---

[2]https://csrc.nist.gov/glossary/term/privileged_user

- Separation of duties

- Role-based access control (RBAC)

- Automate

- Maintain and monitor

- Privileged Access Management combines people, processes, and technology to drastically lower the risk of elevated accounts.

- Chapter 2: Zero Trust: Origins and Evolution

  - Zero Trust is approaching 20 years since it was first coined by John Kindervag, and since then, it has been widely embraced as a critical strategy for reducing cyber risk.

  - Zero Trust is a strategy, not a set of tools or technologies.

  - A vendor does not have an "easy button" to implement it. Some vendors make great tools and technologies as part of their ZT deployment.

  - Because it is a strategy, it requires leadership, scope, and planning for successful deployment and production.

  - Ensure your teams understand vital issues such as the five steps to successful implementation and the three core ZT principles.

  - Lastly, understand that Zero Trust focuses on people, processes, and programs for success, meaning it is a culture shift and, as such, requires solid senior leadership support and engagement.

- Chapter 3: Assessments and Solutions

  - Strategy, Again: It is not enough to list risks; there needs to be a goal or strategy to guide the team to success.

  - Importance of Frameworks: A short discussion of why frameworks are important to the success of cybersecurity.

  - Current State: We discussed a number of ways to assess an organization's current PAM maturity.

  - Assessment and Risk-Based Approach: Taking a risk-based approach is crucial to success as well as having a solid program and project management oversight.

  - Zero Trust Journey Assessment: We discussed some great tools on how to assess a Zero Trust journey that can be leveraged.

Part II: Operationalize

- Chapter 4: PAM Governance

  - Case Studies: Overview of what is involved in making a product PAM environment ready.

  - Small and Medium Businesses: Provided a detailed example of successful PAM implementations in the smallest organizations.

  - Small and Medium Enterprises: Provided a detailed example of different PAM implementations in these medium-sized companies.

  - Large Enterprises: Explained how the largest organizations can accomplish PAM implementations.

- Chapter 5: Blueprint for a Successful Implementation

    - Project Management Methodologies: Incorporated project management methodologies specific to how to deploy PAM.

    - Stakeholder Management: Discussed strategies for managing various stakeholders during implementation.

    - Plan of Action:

        - Planning

        - Execution

        - Governance

        - Root cause analysis

        - Operationalize

        - Metrics for success

    - PAM in DevOps: Discussed the role of PAM in DevOps environments.

    - Human vs. Machine Access: Broke down how PAM/ZT needs to work for human-to-machine access vs. machine-to-machine access. Tied back to identity management (person vs. machine identity).

    - Tools and Technologies: There are a lot of technologies around PAM, and we provided some ways to sort through the jargon and fancy bells and whistles to determine the best fit for your organization.

- PAM for IoT: Explored the challenges and solutions for managing privileged access in IoT and other emerging tech.

- Heavily Regulated: Addressed sector-specific challenges and solutions in PAM implementation.

- Third-Party Access: Discussed the risks and best ways to lower the risk of vendor Privileged Access Management.

- Best Practices and Pitfalls: Shared best practices and common pitfalls across different scenarios.

- Chapter 6: Conclusion

  - This chapter provided two large deliverables: how to build on the success of a PAM deployment by building a learning organization that will continue to improve and learn and a list of resources online for readers to utilize on their own for more help on Privileged Access Management and Zero Trust. The list is long, and as indicated, there is a lot of information already available for use.

Thanks for your purchase of this book, and the authors hope you find it useful and worth the read. Connect with us on LinkedIn and online.

Index

A

Access management process,
4, 6, 15, 20
Access review process, 224
Active Directory (AD), 72
Adverse event analysis
(DE.AE), 116
Agile development
methodology, 216
Amazon Web Services, 219
Application Program Interface
(API), 223, 234
Application-specific actions, 72
Architectural approach, 60
Architecture, 30
Assessment and risk-based
approach
critical, high, medium, and
low, 132
current state, 131
NIST-CSF 2.0, 131
NIST Small Business
Guidance, 131
quantitative approach, 133, 134
risk ranking, 131
target state, 131
Asset management (ID.AM),
108, 109

Assets, 108
Attack Surface *vs.* Protect
Surface, 53
Attribute-Based Access Control, 12
Authentication, 11, 12
Authorization, 12
Automated controls, 59
Automation, 38, 59
Awareness and Training
(PR.AT), 111

B

Biometrics, 12
Brute Force Attack, 12
Business-critical/high-value
application access, 214
Business Impact Analysis (BIA), 179
Business Process Outsourcing
(BPO), 189, 229

C

Case studies
documentation matters, 142
frameworks, 143
guidelines, 142
NIST-CSF Policy Template
Guide, 143

© Gregory C. Rasner, Maria C. Rasner 2025
G. C. Rasner and M. C. Rasner, *Privileged Access Management*,
https://doi.org/10.1007/979-8-8688-1431-0

Z

GPSR Compliance
The European Union's (EU) General Product Safety Regulation (GPSR) is a set
of rules that requires consumer products to be safe and our obligations to
ensure this.

If you have any concerns about our products, you can contact us on

ProductSafety@springernature.com

In case Publisher is established outside the EU, the EU authorized
representative is:

Springer Nature Customer Service Center GmbH
Europaplatz 3
69115 Heidelberg, Germany